THE SMARTEST THINGS EVER SAID

ALSO BY STEVEN D. PRICE

THE
SMARTEST
THINGS EVER
SAID

New and Expanded

Edited and with an introduction by
STEVEN D. PRICE

Guilford, Connecticut

An imprint of Globe Pequot

Distributed by NATIONAL BOOK NETWORK

British Library Cataloguing-in-Publication Information available

Library of Congress Cataloging-in-Publication Data

Names: Price, Steven D., editor.
Title: The smartest things ever said / edited and with an introduction by
  Steven D. Price.
Other titles: 1001 smartest things ever said
Description: New and expanded. | Guilford, Connecticut : Lyons Press, [2017] |
  Includes bibliographical references.
Identifiers: LCCN 2016037276 (print) | LCCN 2016054904 (ebook) | ISBN
  9781493026227 (pbk.) | ISBN 9781493026296 (e-book)
Subjects: LCSH: Quotations, English.
Classification: LCC PN6081 .A126 2017 (print) | LCC PN6081 (ebook) | DDC
  081—dc23
LC record available at https://lccn.loc.gov/2016037276

CONTENTS

I quote others only in order the better to express myself.

—MICHEL DE MONTAIGNE

INTRODUCTION TO THE NEW EDITION

Published a dozen years ago, *1001 Smartest Things Ever Said* was the first of the eight compilations of quotations I've assembled over the years. Just as a parent would be reluctant to single out his or her favorite off-spring, I can't call it mine, but *Smartest* holds a warm spot when I think back to tackling the project. An entire universe awaited, a veritable embarrassment of riches. Alas, that was the problem: although I could have just as easily selected many more quotations that were worthy of inclusion, the publisher asked me to choose only 1,001.

In addition to the original 1,001, this new edition includes 242 more quotations. Some were said or written by contributors to the earlier book, but others come from more contemporary writers, entertainers, politicians, athletes, clergy, and other figures whom most of us were unaware of or barely familiar with a dozen years ago. That there is no time limit to wise utterances is reassuring in these troubled times.

A category of quotations to which I'm particularly drawn is proverbs. Their very nature implies a lack of originality, but to view them as time-worn clichés is to miss the point. Any proverb lacking distilled folk wisdom that speaks to new generations with renewed vigor would have disappeared through the very same folk process by which they were created.

The quotations between these covers encompass every human situation and activity. Reflections on "Life and Death (And Some of What Happens in Between)" span from the cradle to the grave. "The Life of the Mind" examines the intellectual, while interpersonal relationships are the subject of "Love and Friendship." Both the spiritual and the worldly figure prominently in "Success, and Ways to Achieve It" and "Politics and Politicians, Government and Statesmen." "Proverbial Wisdom" is a concentration of just that, although many other proverbs appear where and when especially relevant in other chapters.

The contributors consist of no less a wide range. John Donne and Mick Jagger, Louis C.K. and J. K. Rowling, Mother Teresa and Marilyn Monroe, Barack Obama and Yogi Berra—strange bedfellows perhaps, but that simply demonstrates that there is no monopoly on wisdom.

Which entry in the entire book qualifies as the smartest? Although wisdom is seldom a competition sport, that's a question I've been asked, and more than once, and I continue to hark back to the memory of a television drama from the 1950s, on a series that older readers may recall as "Four Star Playhouse." The setting was a bar into which a group of people had wandered to seek companionship in face of the world's coming to an end (I can't recall how or why, but Armageddon was nigh). One of the patrons had a computer—very much a novelty sixty years ago—into which he had entered all of the world's literature. Surrounded by the other patrons, he then asked the computer to answer the question, "How can the world be saved?"

After much whirring of gears and flashing of keyboard lights (remember, this was the '50s), the answer began: "I am the Lord Thy God; Thou shalt have no other god before me. . . ." and thereafter followed the rest of the Ten Commandments. One TV scriptwriter's opinion, but certainly food for thought. (So's the fact that the Golden Rule appears in almost every culture and faith on this planet.)

Much has changed in the past sixty years. True wisdom, however, does not because truth abideth forever. In a society that continues to be accused of taking dumbing-down to new heights (or depths), studying the wisdom of the ages is a vital step in maintaining—and regaining—intellectual and ethical standards.

—Steven D. Price
2017

I.

Life and Death
(And Some of What Happens
in Between)

Life can only be understood backwards; but it must be lived forwards.

—SØREN KIERKEGAARD

There is no cure for birth and death save to enjoy the interval.

—GEORGE SANTAYANA

The future you shall know when it has come; before then forget it.

—AESCHYLUS

One's own thought is one's world.

What a person thinks is what he becomes.

—MAITRI UPANISHADS

Time ripens all things; no man is born wise.
—MIGUEL DE CERVANTES

A baby is God's opinion that life should go on.
—CARL SANDBURG

It is easier for a father to have children than
for children to have a real father.
—POPE JOHN XXIII

The most important question in the world is,
"Why is the child crying?"
—ALICE WALKER

If you can give your son or daughter only one gift, let it be enthusiasm.
—BRUCE BARTON

If there is anything we wish to change in the child,
we should first examine it and see whether it is not
something that could better be changed in ourselves.
—CARL JUNG

Ain't no man can avoid being born average,
but there ain't no man got to be common.
—SATCHEL PAIGE

I am afraid we must make the world honest before we can
honestly say to our children that honesty is the best policy.
—SIR WALTER BESANT

You can learn many things from children.

How much patience you have, for instance.

—FRANKLIN P. ADAMS

•

Acting childish seems to come naturally, but acting like an adult,

no matter how old we are, just doesn't come easy to us.

—LILY TOMLIN

•

My father always said there are four things a child needs: plenty

of love, nourishing food, regular sleep, and lots of soap and water.

After that, what he needs most is some intelligent neglect.

—IVY BAKER PRIEST

•

A birthday is a good time to begin anew: throwing away the old

habits, as you would old clothes, and never putting them on again.

—BRONSON ALCOTT

Growth is the only evidence of life.
—JOHN HENRY NEWMAN

•

The hardest thing to learn in life is which
bridge to cross and which to burn.
—DAVID RUSSELL

•

Some people are so much sunshine to the square inch.
—WALT WHITMAN

•

The most difficult thing in the world is to know how to do a thing
and to watch someone else do it wrong, without comment.
—T. H. WHITE

"If everybody minded their own business," the Duchess said in a hoarse growl, "the world would go round a good deal faster than it does."
— LEWIS CARROLL

Live a life as a monument to your soul.
— AYN RAND

If you're in a card game and you don't know who the sucker is, you're it.
— ANONYMOUS

Too many people are thinking of security instead of opportunity.
They seem more afraid of life than death.
— JAMES F. BYRNES

We boil at different degrees.

—RALPH WALDO EMERSON

•

I would feel more optimistic about a bright future for man if he spent less time proving that he can outwit Nature and more time tasting her sweetness and respecting her seniority.

—E. B. WHITE

•

No man is a hero to his own valet.

—ANONYMOUS

•

Men occasionally stumble over the truth, but most of them pick themselves up and hurry on as if nothing had happened.

—SIR WINSTON CHURCHILL

Service to others is the rent you pay for your room here on earth.

—MUHAMMAD ALI

The best and safest thing is to keep a balance in your life,
acknowledge the great powers around us and in us. If you can
do that, and live that way, you are really a wise man.

—EURIPIDES

Life is a great big canvas; throw all the paint you can at it.

—DANNY KAYE

You gain strength, courage and confidence by every experience in which you really stop to look fear in the face. You are able to say to yourself, "I lived through this horror. I can take the next thing that comes along."

—ELEANOR ROOSEVELT

•

The point of music is discovered in every moment of playing and listening to it. It is the same, I feel, with the greater part of our lives, and if we are unduly absorbed in improving them we may forget altogether to live them.

—ALAN B. WATTS

•

Nearly all men can stand adversity, but if you want to test a man's character, give him power.

—ABRAHAM LINCOLN

On the whole, human beings want to be good,

but not too good and not quite all the time.

—GEORGE ORWELL

•

This above all: to thine own self be true,

And it must follow, as the night the day,

Thou canst not then be false to any man.

—WILLIAM SHAKESPEARE

•

Know how sublime a thing is to suffer and be strong.

—HENRY WADSWORTH LONGFELLOW

•

Be more concerned with your character than your reputation,

because your character is what you really are, while your

reputation is merely what others think you are.

—JOHN R. WOODEN

Education is the best provision for the journey to old age.

—ARISTOTLE

I am never afraid of what I know.

—ANNA SEWELL

Never be haughty to the humble; never be humble to the haughty.

—JEFFERSON DAVIS

It is extraordinary how extraordinary the ordinary person is.

—GEORGE F. WILL

The majority of men are bundles of beginnings.
—**RALPH WALDO EMERSON**

Contemplate thy powers, contemplate thy wants and thy connections;
so shalt thou discover the duties of life, and be directed in all thy ways.
—**AKHENATEN**

The childhood shows the man, as morning shows the day.
—**JOHN MILTON**

The young always have the same problem—how to rebel
and conform at the same time. They have solved this by
defying their parents and copying one another.
—**QUENTIN CRISP**

Who does not grow, declines.
—RABBI HILLEL

•

There is no reason why the same man should
like the same book at 18 and at 48.
—EZRA POUND

•

The man who views the world at 50 the same as he
did at 20 has wasted thirty years of his life.
—MUHAMMAD ALI

•

If all misfortunes were laid in one common heap whence
everyone must take an equal portion, most people would
be contented to take their own and depart.
—SOCRATES

Many people genuinely do not wish to be saints, and it is possible that some who achieve or aspire to sainthood have never had much temptation to be human beings.
—GEORGE ORWELL

Don't judge each day by the harvest you reap,
but by the seeds you plant.
—ROBERT LOUIS STEVENSON

If you can spend a perfectly useless afternoon in a perfectly useless manner, you have learned how to live.
—LIN YUTANG

The man who insists upon seeing with perfect clearness before he decides, never decides. Accept life, and you must accept regret.
—HENRI-FRÉDÉRIC AMIEL

He has great tranquility of heart who cares neither
for the praises nor the fault-finding of men.
—HONORÉ DE BALZAC

•

One reason why birds and horses are not unhappy is because
they are not trying to impress other birds and horses.
—DALE CARNEGIE

•

To say yes, you have to sweat and roll up your sleeves
and plunge both hands into life up to the elbows.
It's easy to say no, even if it means dying.
—JEAN ANOUILH

•

A dead thing can go with the stream,
but only a living thing can go against it.
—G. K. CHESTERTON

When you are younger you get blamed for crimes you never
committed and when you're older you begin to get credit
for virtues you never possessed. It evens itself out.

— GEORGE SANTAYANA

Life is an echo. What you send out—you get back.
What you give—you get.

— ANONYMOUS

Life is like playing a violin in public and learning
the instrument as one goes on.

— SAMUEL BUTLER

Life consists not in holding good cards but
in playing those you hold well.

— JOSH BILLINGS

Life is an adventure in forgiveness.
—NORMAN COUSINS

•

Life is the art of drawing sufficient conclusions
from insufficient premises.
—SAMUEL BUTLER

•

If you can't make it better, you can laugh at it.
—ERMA BOMBECK

•

Character is much easier kept than recovered.
—THOMAS PAINE

This is the first test of a gentleman: his respect for
those who can be of no possible value to him.
—**WILLIAM LYON PHELPS**

The future comes one day at a time.
—**DEAN ACHESON**

Do well and you will have no need for ancestors.
—**VOLTAIRE**

The strongest man in the world is he who stands alone.
—**HENRIK IBSEN**

All life is 6 to 5 against.

—**DAMON RUNYON**

The measure of a man is the way he bears up under misfortune.

—**PLUTARCH**

Hope springs eternal in the human breast: /
Man never is, but always to be blest.

—**ALEXANDER POPE**

A mature person is one who does not think only in absolutes,
who is able to be objective even when deeply stirred
emotionally, who has learned that there is both good and
bad in all people and all things, and who walks humbly
and deals charitably with the circumstances of life.

—**ELEANOR ROOSEVELT**

The moment we begin to fear the opinions of others and
hesitate to tell the truth that is in us, and from motives
of policy are silent when we should speak, the divine
floods of light and life no longer flow into our souls.
—ELIZABETH CADY STANTON

It is not only for what we do that we are held
responsible, but also for what we do not do.
—MOLIÈRE

People travel to wonder at the height of the mountains,
at the huge waves of the seas, at the long course of the rivers,
at the vast compass of the ocean, at the circular motion of the
stars, and yet they pass by themselves without wondering.
—SAINT AUGUSTINE

Time is the wisest counselor.

—PERICLES

Happy the man, and happy he alone,

He who can call today his own:

He who, secure within, can say,

Tomorrow do thy worst, for I have lived today.

Be fair or foul or rain or shine

The joys I have possessed, in spite of fate, are mine.

Not Heaven itself upon the past has power,

But what has been, has been, and I have had my hour.

—HORACE

The older I grow the more I distrust the familiar

doctrine that age brings wisdom.

—H. L. MENCKEN

Go confidently in the direction of your dreams!
Live the life you've imagined. As you simplify your
life, the laws of the universe will be simpler.
—**HENRY DAVID THOREAU**

●

I do not believe that sheer suffering teaches. If suffering alone
taught, all the world would be wise, since everyone suffers. To
suffering must be added mourning, understanding, patience,
love, openness and the willingness to remain vulnerable.
—**JOSEPH ADDISON**

●

Before I can live with other folks I've got to live with myself. The one
thing that doesn't abide by majority rule is a person's conscience.
—**HARPER LEE**

Never feel self-pity, the most destructive emotion there is.
How awful to be caught up in the terrible squirrel cage of self.
—MILLICENT FENWICK

A halo has to fall only a few inches to be a noose.
—ANONYMOUS

If you cry because the sun has gone out of your life,
your tears will prevent you from seeing the stars.
—RABINDRANATH TAGORE

A man's heart away from nature becomes hard; lack of respect for
growing, living things soon leads to a lack of respect for humans too.
—LUTHER STANDING BEAR

Happiness is always a by-product. It is probably a matter of temperament, and for anything I know it may be glandular. But it is not something that can be demanded from life, and if you are not happy you had better stop worrying about it.

—ROBERTSON DAVIES

Live your questions now, and perhaps even without knowing it, you will live along some distant day into your answers.

—RAINER MARIA RILKE

Be grateful for luck. Pay the thunder no mind— listen to the birds. And don't hate nobody.

—EUBIE BLAKE

May you have a strong foundation when the winds of
changes shift . . . and may you be forever young.
—BOB DYLAN

•

Do not go where the path may lead, go instead
where there is no path and leave a trail.
—RALPH WALDO EMERSON

•

Growth demands a temporary surrender of security.
—GAIL SHEEHY

•

The mass of men lead lives of quiet desperation.
—HENRY DAVID THOREAU

Reflect upon your present blessings, of which every man has plenty;

not on your past misfortunes of which all men have some.

—CHARLES DICKENS

Never let yesterday use up too much of today.

—WILL ROGERS

I can resist everything except temptation.

—OSCAR WILDE

To succeed in life, you need two things: ignorance and confidence.

—MARK TWAIN

Expect nothing. Live frugally on surprise.
—ALICE WALKER

A man cannot be too careful in his choice of enemies.
—OSCAR WILDE

A great secret of success is to go through life

as a man who never gets used up.
—ALBERT SCHWEITZER

Just trust yourself, then you will know how to live.
—JOHANN WOLFGANG VON GOETHE

A man of good will with a little effort and belief in his
own powers can enjoy a deep, tranquil, rich life—provided
he go his own way. . . . To live one's own life is still the
best way of life, always was, and always will be.
— HENRY MILLER

If only I may grow: firmer, simpler—quieter, warmer.
— DAG HAMMARSKJÖLD

You can outdistance that which is running after
you, but not what is running inside you.
— RWANDAN PROVERB

This existence of ours is as transient as autumn clouds.
To watch the birth and death of beings is like looking at the
movements of a dance. A lifetime is a flash of lightning in the
sky. Rushing by, like a torrent down a steep mountain.
—BUDDHA

We are here to laugh at the odds and live our lives
so well that Death will tremble to take us.
—CHARLES BUKOWSKI

Death is nothing to us, since when we are, death has
not come, and when death has come, we are not.
—EPICURUS

We are no more than candles burning in the wind.
—JAPANESE PROVERB

Live so that you wouldn't be ashamed to sell

the family parrot to the town gossip.

—WILL ROGERS

All would live long, but none would be old.

—BENJAMIN FRANKLIN

It is in self-limitation that a master first shows himself.

—JOHANN WOLFGANG VON GOETHE

In the long run, we shape our lives, and we shape ourselves.

The process never ends until we die. And the choices

we make are ultimately our own responsibility.

—ELEANOR ROOSEVELT

The mere process of growing old together will make

the slightest acquaintance seem a bosom friend.

—LOGAN PEARSALL SMITH

•

You are never too old to be what you might have been.

—GEORGE ELIOT

•

If I knew I was going to live this long, I'd

have taken better care of myself.

—MICKEY MANTLE

•

I went to the woods because I wished to live deliberately, to front only

the essential facts of life and see if I could not learn what they had to

teach; and not, when I came to die, discover that I had not lived.

—HENRY DAVID THOREAU, *WALDEN*

People—some good, some bad, but in the long run we come out even.

—JAN HITTLE

●

The trouble with quotes about death is that 99.999 percent

of them are made by people who are still alive.

—JOSHUA BRUNS

●

As a well-spent day brings happy sleep,

so a life well spent brings happy death.

—LEONARDO DA VINCI

●

In an artist's life, death is perhaps not the most difficult thing.

—VINCENT VAN GOGH

Death—the last sleep? No, it is the final awakening.
—**SIR WALTER SCOTT**

•

Lord, how the day passes! It's like a life—so quickly
when we don't watch it and so slowly if we do.
—**JOHN STEINBECK**

•

I have discovered that all human evil comes from this: man's
being unable to sit still and quiet in a room alone.
—**BLAISE PASCAL**

It is said an Eastern monarch once charged his wise men to invent him a sentence, to be ever in view, and which should be true and appropriate in all times and situations. They presented him the words: And this, too, shall pass away.

—ABRAHAM LINCOLN

No man is an Island, entire of itself; every man is a piece of the Continent, a part of the main; if a clod be washed away by the sea, Europe is the less, as well as if a promontory were, as well as if a manor of thy friends or of thine own were; any man's death diminishes me, because I am involved in Mankind; And therefore never send to know for whom the bell tolls; It tolls for thee.

—JOHN DONNE

I want to live my life so that my nights are not full of regrets.

—D. H. LAWRENCE

I promise to keep on living as though I expected to live forever. Nobody grows old by merely living a number of years. People grow old by deserting their ideals. Years may wrinkle the skin, but to give up wrinkles the soul.

—DOUGLAS MACARTHUR

•

May you live all the days of your life.

—JONATHAN SWIFT

•

Live simply, that others may simply live.

—MOHANDAS GANDHI

•

Keep on truckin'.

—ROBERT CRUMB

Hope is a good breakfast, but it is a bad supper.

—SIR FRANCIS BACON

My advice to you is not to inquire why or whither, but just enjoy

your ice cream while it's on your plate—that's my philosophy.

—THORNTON WILDER

Enjoy the spring of love and youth,

To some good angel leave the rest;

For time will teach thee soon the truth,

There are no birds in last year's nest.

—HENRY WADSWORTH LONGFELLOW

Know the true value of time; snatch, seize, and enjoy every
moment of it. No idleness, no laziness, no procrastination:
never put off till to-morrow what you can do to-day.
—PHILIP DORMER STANHOPE, LORD CHESTERFIELD

Let us not look back in anger, nor forward
in fear, but around in awareness.
—JAMES THURBER

Experience is a hard teacher. She gives the
test first and the lessons afterwards.
—ANONYMOUS

No man is rich enough to buy back his past.
—OSCAR WILDE

In times like these, it helps to recall that there

have always been times like these.

—PAUL HARVEY

Make voyages! Attempt them . . . there's nothing else.

—TENNESSEE WILLIAMS

The best portion of a good man's life is his little, nameless,

unremembered acts of kindness and of love.

—WILLIAM WORDSWORTH

The years between fifty and seventy are the hardest.

You are always being asked to do things, and yet you

are not decrepit enough to turn them down.

—T. S. ELIOT

Men are like wine—some turn to vinegar,

but the best improve with age.

—POPE JOHN XXIII

Grow old along with me! / The best is yet to be.

—ROBERT BROWNING

The only man who behaves sensibly is my tailor; he takes my

measure anew every time he sees me, whilst all the rest go on

with their old measurements, and expect them to fit me.

—GEORGE BERNARD SHAW

One of the secrets of a long and fruitful life is to forgive
everybody everything every night before you go to bed.
—BERNARD MANNES BARUCH

Old age ain't no place for sissies.
—BETTE DAVIS

Don't look back. Something might be gaining on you.
—SATCHEL PAIGE

Don't hurry, don't worry. You're here for a short visit.
So be sure to stop and smell the flowers.
—WALTER HAGEN

Live as long as you can. Die when you can't help it.

—JAMES BROWN

•

A person will be called to account on Judgment Day for every permissible thing he might have enjoyed but did not.

—THE TALMUD

•

Millions long for immortality who do not know what to do with themselves on a rainy Sunday afternoon.

—SUSAN ERTZ

•

Old age is like everything else. To make a success of it, you've got to start young.

—FRED ASTAIRE

Since time is not a person we can overtake when he is past, let us honor him with mirth and cheerfulness of heart while he is passing.
—**JOHANN WOLFGANG VON GOETHE**

•

I shall tell you a great secret, my friend. Do not wait for the last judgement, it takes place every day.
—**ALBERT CAMUS**

•

To be idle is a short road to death and to be diligent is a way of life; foolish people are idle, wise people are diligent.
—**BUDDHA**

•

I have an irrepressible desire to live till I can be assured that the world is a little better for my having lived in it.
—**ABRAHAM LINCOLN**

Man is the only animal that blushes. Or needs to.
—**MARK TWAIN**

The tragedy of life is not so much what men
suffer, but rather what they miss.
—**THOMAS CARLYLE**

The greatest thing in life is to die young—
but delay it as long as possible.
—**GEORGE BERNARD SHAW**

I like living. I have sometimes been wildly, despairingly,
acutely miserable, racked with sorrow, but through it all I still
know quite certainly that just to be alive is a grand thing.
—**AGATHA CHRISTIE**

Taking joy in life is a woman's best cosmetic.
—**ROSALIND RUSSELL**

•

The greatest pleasure in life is doing what people say you cannot do.
—**WALTER BAGEHOT**

•

The difference between life and the movies is that
a script has to make sense, and life doesn't.
—**JOSEPH L. MANKIEWICZ**

•

Never, never rest contented with any circle of ideas, but
always be certain that a wider one is still possible.
—**PEARL BAILEY**

It is hard to have patience with people who say "There is no death" or "Death doesn't matter." There is death. And whatever is matters. And whatever happens has consequences, and it and they are irrevocable and irreversible. You might as well say that birth doesn't matter.

—C. S. LEWIS

Judge a man by his questions rather than his answers.

—VOLTAIRE

Things are seldom what they seem.

—SIR WILLIAM S. GILBERT

Good advice is something a man gives when he is too old to set a bad example.

—FRANÇOIS DE LA ROCHEFOUCAULD

The bitterest tears shed over graves are for words
left unsaid and deeds left undone.
—HARRIET BEECHER STOWE

God not only plays dice, he throws them in
the corner where you can't see them.
—STEPHEN HAWKING

There is, therefore, only one categorical imperative. It is:
Act only according to that maxim by which you can at the
same time will that it should become a universal law.
—IMMANUEL KANT

How wonderful it is that nobody need wait a single

moment before starting to improve the world.

—ANNE FRANK

•

What the superior man seeks is in himself.

What the mean man seeks is in others.

—CONFUCIUS

•

Courage is contagious. When a brave man takes

a stand, the spines of others are stiffened.

—BILLY GRAHAM

•

Lying to ourselves is more deeply ingrained than lying to others.

—FYODOR MIKHAILOVICH DOSTOYEVSKY

Cowards die many times before their deaths;

The valiant never taste death but once.

—WILLIAM SHAKESPEARE

Hateful to me as the gates of Hades is that man who

hides one thing in his heart and speaks another.

—HOMER

Your vision will become clear only when you can look into your

own heart. Who looks outside, dreams; who looks inside, awakens.

—CARL JUNG

It is a human nature to think wisely and act foolishly.

—ANATOLE FRANCE

Everything should be as simple as it is, but not simpler.
—ALBERT EINSTEIN

•

A man has to live with himself, and he should see

to it that he always has good company.
—CHARLES EVANS HUGHES

•

Wealth and children are the adornment of this present life,

but good works, which are lasting, are better in the sight

of thy Lord as to recompense, and better as to hope.
—THE KORAN

•

If you enjoy living, it is not difficult to keep the sense of wonder.
—RAY BRADBURY

Words make you think a thought. Music makes you
feel a feeling. A song makes you feel a thought.
—E. Y. HARBURG

Worry is like a rocking chair, it will give you something
to do, but it won't get you anywhere.
—ANONYMOUS

Silence is argument carried on by other means.
—ERNESTO "CHE" GUEVARA

To do just the opposite is also a form of imitation.
—GEORG CHRISTOPH LICHTENBERG

The gentle mind by gentle deeds is known. For a man
by nothing is so well betrayed, as by his manners.
—EDMUND SPENSER

•

He who angers you conquers you.
—ELIZABETH KENNY

•

Believe not because some old manuscripts are produced,
believe not because it is your national belief, believe not because you
have been made to believe from your childhood, but reason truth
out, and after you have analyzed it, then if you find it will do good
to one and all, believe it, live up to it and help others live up to it.
—BUDDHA

The line dividing good and evil cuts through the heart of every human being. And who is willing to destroy a piece of his own heart?
—ALEKSANDR SOLZHENITSYN

He who forgiveth, and is reconciled unto his enemy, shall receive his reward from God; for he loveth not the unjust doers.
—THE KORAN

Let us then suppose the mind to be, as we say, a white paper, void of all characters, without any ideas. How comes it to be furnished? . . . To this I answer, in one word, from experience.
—JOHN LOCKE

He that troubleth his own house shall inherit the wind.
—THE BIBLE, PROVERBS 11:29

Everyone can master a grief but he that has it.
—**WILLIAM SHAKESPEARE**

•

As through this world I rambled

I've seen lots of funny men.

Some will rob you with a six-gun

And some with a fountain pen.
—**WOODY GUTHRIE**

•

As blushing will sometimes make a whore pass for a virtuous

woman, so modesty may make a fool seem a man of sense.
—**JONATHAN SWIFT**

•

Without music, life is a journey through a desert.
—**PAT CONROY**

Sooner or later we all discover that the important moments in life are not the advertised ones, not the birthdays, the graduations, the weddings, not the great goals achieved. The real milestones are less prepossessing. They come to the door of memory unannounced, stray dogs that amble in, sniff around a bit and simply never leave. Our lives are measured by these.
—SUSAN B. ANTHONY

•

Use your health, even to the point of wearing it out. That is what it is for. Spend all you have before you die; and do not outlive yourself.
—GEORGE BERNARD SHAW

•

Whoever destroys a single life is as guilty as though he had destroyed the entire world; and whoever rescues a single life earns as much merit as though he had rescued the entire world.
—THE TALMUD

Age is a question of mind over matter.

If you don't mind, it doesn't matter.

—SATCHEL PAIGE

•

For of all sad words of tongue or pen /

the saddest are these; It might have been!

—JOHN GREENLEAF WHITTIER

•

A thing is not necessarily true because a man dies for it.

—OSCAR WILDE

•

Wrinkles should merely indicate where smiles have been.

—MARK TWAIN

Growing old is no more than a bad habit that
a busy person has not time to form.
— **ANDRÉ MAUROIS**

If you think about disaster, you will get it. Brood about death
and you hasten your demise. Think positively and masterfully,
with confidence and faith, and life becomes more secure, more
fraught with action, richer in achievement and experience.
— **SWAMI SIVANANDA**

The act of dying is also one of the acts of life.
— **MARCUS AURELIUS**

The Moving Finger writes; and having writ,
Moves on; nor all your Piety nor Wit
Shall lure it back to cancel half a Line,
Nor all your Tears wash out a Word of it.
— **OMAR KHAYYAM**

Old age is far more than white hair, wrinkles, the feeling
that it is too late and the game finished, that the stage
belongs to the rising generations. The true evil is not the
weakening of the body, but the indifference of the soul.
—ANDRÉ MAUROIS

•

When you're young and you fall off a horse, you may break
something. When you're my age and you fall off, you splatter.
—ROY ROGERS

•

When the great scorer comes to write against your name, he
marks not that you won or lost, but how you played the game.
—GRANTLAND RICE

•

A lifetime of happiness! No man alive could bear it:
it would be hell on earth.
—GEORGE BERNARD SHAW

Old minds are like old horses; you must exercise them
if you wish to keep them in working order.
— JOHN ADAMS

I wasted time, and now doth time waste me.
— WILLIAM SHAKESPEARE

Anyone who keeps the ability to see beauty in
every age of life really never grows old.
— FRANZ KAFKA

Life is like a game of cards. The hand you are dealt is
determinism; the way you play it is free will.
— JAWAHARLAL NEHRU

We can easily forgive a child who is afraid of the dark.
The real tragedy of life is when men are afraid of the light.
—PLATO

•

And we should consider every day lost on which we have
not danced at least once. And we should call every truth
false which was not accompanied by at least one laugh.
—FRIEDRICH WILHELM NIETZSCHE

•

We don't see things as they are, we see them as we are.
—ANAÏS NIN

•

The happy man is not he who seems thus to
others, but who seems thus to himself.
—MARCEL PROUST

When you betray somebody else, you also betray yourself.
—ISAAC BASHEVIS SINGER

No matter how dark things seem to be or actually are, raise your sights
and see the possibilities—always see them, for they're always there.
—NORMAN VINCENT PEALE

In order for three people to keep a secret, two must be dead.
—BENJAMIN FRANKLIN

In the majority of sane human lives there is no problem of
sex at all; there is no problem of marriage at all; there is no
problem of temperament at all; for all these problems are
dwarfed and rendered ridiculous by the standing problem of
being a moderately honest man and paying the butcher.
—G. K. CHESTERTON

Three o'clock is always too late or too early

for anything you want to do.

—JEAN-PAUL SARTRE

•

My hopes are not always realized, but I always hope.

—OVID

•

Sometimes a cigar is just a cigar.

—SIGMUND FREUD

•

All is for the best in the best of all possible worlds.

—VOLTAIRE

Whatever befalls the earth befalls the sons and daughters of the earth. We did not weave the web of life; We are merely a strand in it. What we do with the web, we do to ourselves . . .
—CHIEF SEATTLE

The world is full of magical things patiently waiting for our wits to grow sharper.
—BERTRAND RUSSELL

The best remedy for anger is delay.
—BRIGHAM YOUNG

Live well. It is the greatest revenge.
—THE TALMUD

A ship ought not to be held by one anchor, nor life by a single hope.

— EPICTETUS

•

I keep my ideals, because in spite of everything I still

believe that people are really good at heart.

— ANNE FRANK

•

A community is like a ship, everyone ought

to be prepared to take the helm.

— HENRIK IBSEN

•

Sometimes our light goes out but is blown into flame

by another human being. Each of us owes deepest

thanks to those who have rekindled this light.

— ALBERT SCHWEITZER

Life does not cease to be funny when people die any more
than it ceases to be serious when people laugh.
—ANTOINE DE SAINT-EXUPÉRY

Desire is half of life, indifference is half of death.
—KAHLIL GIBRAN

Life is pleasant. Death is peaceful. It's the transition that's troublesome.
—ISAAC ASIMOV

The great consolation in life is to say what one thinks.
—VOLTAIRE

Men fear death, as children fear to go in the dark; and as that natural fear in children is increased with tales, so is the other.
—SIR FRANCIS BACON

If man hasn't discovered something that he will die for, he isn't fit to live.
—MARTIN LUTHER KING JR.

Death is not extinguishing the light; it is putting out the lamp because dawn has come.
—RABINDRANATH TAGORE

Be of good cheer about death and know this as a truth— that no evil can happen to a good man, either in life or after death.
—SOCRATES

I said to Life, "I would hear Death speak." And Life raised
her voice a little higher and said, "You hear him now."
—**KAHLIL GIBRAN**

•

The riders in a race do not stop short when they reach the
goal. There is a little finishing canter before they come to a
standstill. . . . The canter that brings you to a standstill need
not be only coming to rest. It cannot be while you still live.
—**OLIVER WENDELL HOLMES JR.**

•

Our fear of death is like our fear that summer will be short,
but when we have had our swing of pleasure, our fill of fruit,
and our swelter of heat, we say we have had our day.
—**RALPH WALDO EMERSON**

Sweet is a grief well ended.

—AESCHYLUS

•

To be able to look back upon one's life in satisfaction, is to live twice.

—KAHLIL GIBRAN

•

It's not over until it's over.

—YOGI BERRA

•

When I look back on all these worries, I remember the story
of the old man who said on his deathbed that he had had a lot
of trouble in his life, most of which had never happened.

—SIR WINSTON CHURCHILL

Neither fire nor wind, birth nor death can erase our good deeds.

—**BUDDHA**

Death ends a life, not a relationship.

—**JACK LEMMON**

I decline to accept the end of man. It is easy enough to say that man is immortal because he will endure: that when the last ding-dong of doom has clanged and faded from the last worthless rock hanging tideless in the last red and dying evening, that even then there will still be one more sound: that of his puny inexhaustible voice, still talking. I refuse to accept this. I believe that man will not merely endure: he will prevail. He is immortal, not because he alone among creatures has an inexhaustible voice, but because he has a soul, a spirit capable of compassion and sacrifice and endurance.

—**WILLIAM FAULKNER**

Fear not for the future, weep not for the past.
—PERCY BYSSHE SHELLEY

I speak truth, not so much as I would, but as much as
I dare; and I dare a little more, as I grow older.
—CATHERINE DRINKER BOWEN

How far you go in life depends on your being tender with
the young, compassionate with the aged, sympathetic with
the striving, and tolerant of the weak and strong. Because
someday in your life you will have been all of these.
—GEORGE WASHINGTON CARVER

I always remember an epitaph which is in the cemetery at
Tombstone, Arizona. It says: "Here lies Jack Williams. He done his
damnedest." I think that is the greatest epitaph a man can have.
—HARRY S. TRUMAN

In the end, everything is a gag.
—CHARLIE CHAPLIN

In three words I can sum up everything I've
learned about life: it goes on.
—ROBERT FROST

Tough times don't last, tough people do.
—ROBERT H. SCHULLER

Life is what we make it, always has been, always will be.
—ANNA MARY ROBERTSON ("GRANDMA") MOSES

"It's no use going back to yesterday," [Alice said,]

"because I was a different person then."

—LEWIS CARROLL

Half the fun of nearly everything, you know, is

thinking about it beforehand, or afterward.

—HOWARD R. GARIS

Experience keeps a dear school, but fools will

learn in no other, and scarce in that.

—BENJAMIN FRANKLIN

There are two things to aim at in life: first, to get what you want; and,

after that, to enjoy it. Only the wisest of mankind achieve the second.

—LOGAN PEARSALL SMITH

You just hold your head high and keep those fists down.
No matter what anyone says to you, don't let 'em get your
goat. Try fighting with your head for a change . . .
—HARPER LEE

Anyone can carry his burden, however hard, until nightfall.
Anyone can do his work, however hard, for one day.
Anyone can live sweetly, patiently, lovingly, purely, till
the sun goes down. And this is all life really means.
—ROBERT LOUIS STEVENSON

We have always held to the hope, the belief, the conviction
that there is a better life, a better world, beyond the horizon.
—FRANKLIN DELANO ROOSEVELT

Bloom where you are planted.
—THE BIBLE, 1 CORINTHIANS 7:20−24

No act of kindness, no matter how small, is ever wasted.
—AESOP, "THE LION AND THE MOUSE"

•

Nobody made a greater mistake than he who did
nothing because he could do only a little.
—EDMUND BURKE

•

The noblest question in the world is, What good may I do in it?
—BENJAMIN FRANKLIN

•

There are two kinds of light—the glow that
illuminates, and the glare that obscures.
—JAMES THURBER

It is not enough to be industrious; so are the
ants. What are you industrious about?
—HENRY DAVID THOREAU

Do one thing every day that scares you.
—ELEANOR ROOSEVELT

If I were asked to give what I consider the single most useful bit of
advice for all humanity it would be this: Expect trouble as an inevitable
part of life and when it comes, hold you head high, look it squarely
in eye and say, "I will be bigger than you. You cannot defeat me."
—ANN LANDERS

Be still like a mountain and flow like a great river.

—LAO-TZU

•

There's only one rule that I know of, babies—
"God damn it, you've got to be kind."

—KURT VONNEGUT

•

The meaning of life is to find your gift. The
purpose of life is to give it away.

—SOURCE UNKNOWN

•

It is better to sleep on things beforehand than
lie awake about them afterwards.

—BALTASAR GRACIÁN

Each year one vicious habit rooted out in time might

make the worst man good throughout.

—BENJAMIN FRANKLIN

•

A man is rich in proportion to the number of

things he can afford to let alone.

—HENRY DAVID THOREAU

•

Those who think they have no time for exercise will

sooner or later have to find time for illness.

—EDWARD STANLEY

•

Today is the oldest you've ever been, and

the youngest you'll ever be again.

—ELEANOR ROOSEVELT

The answer to old age is to keep one's mind busy and
to go on with one's life as if it were interminable.
—**LEON EDEL**

•

Life is a dream for the wise, a game for the fool,
a comedy for the rich, a tragedy for the poor.
—**SHOLEM ALEICHEM**

•

What do we live for if not to make life less difficult for each other?
—**GEORGE ELIOT**

•

Light tomorrow with today.
—**ELIZABETH BARRETT BROWNING**

If you would reap praise, you must sow the seeds,

gentle words, and useful deeds.

—BENJAMIN FRANKLIN

Every one should keep a mental wastepaper basket
and the older he grows the more things he will
consign to it—torn up to irrecoverable tatters.

—SAMUEL BUTLER

Do what you can, with what you have, where you are.

—THEODORE ROOSEVELT

Good for the body is the work of the body, and good for the soul is
the work of the soul, and good for either is the work of the other.
— **HENRY DAVID THOREAU**

•

Today is life—the only life you are sure of. Make the most of today.
Get interested in something. Shake yourself awake. Develop a hobby.
Let the winds of enthusiasm sweep through you. Live today with gusto.
— **DALE CARNEGIE**

•

It does not do to dwell on dreams and forget to live, remember that.
— **J. K. ROWLING**

•

I would strongly advise you to make up your mind, shoulder your gun,
muster all your spirits, and start in search of the interesting unknown.
— **JOHN JAMES AUDUBON**

Parents can only give good advice or put them on the right paths,
but the final forming of a person's character lies in their own hands.
—ANNE FRANK

The first principle is that you must not fool yourself,
and you're the easiest person to fool.
—RICHARD FEYNMAN

There is something enormously fulfilling about being engaged in
something bigger than you yourself. It imparts a satisfying sense of
purpose which, in my experience, is not attained in any other way.
—GENERAL BRENT SCOWCROFT

Sometimes it's more important to be human than to have good taste.
—BERTOLT BRECHT

We are taxed twice as much by our idleness, three times as
much by our pride, and four times as much by our folly.
—BENJAMIN FRANKLIN

•

Life shrinks or expands in proportion to one's courage.
—ANAÏS NIN

•

My dear, here we must run as fast as we can, just to stay in place.
And if you wish to go anywhere you must run twice as fast as that.
—LEWIS CARROLL

•

Dignity does not come from avenging insults, especially from
violence that can never be justified. It comes from taking
responsibility and advancing our common humanity.
—HILLARY RODHAM CLINTON

Life is a daring adventure or nothing at all.
—HELEN KELLER

•

I always wondered why somebody didn't do something
about that. Then I realized I was somebody.
—LILY TOMLIN

•

How can we expect our children to know and experience the
joy of giving unless we teach them that the greater pleasure
in life lies in the art of giving rather than receiving?
—JAMES CASH PENNEY

Treat people as if they were what they ought to be, and help them become what they are capable of being.
— JOHANN WOLFGANG VON GOETHE

Never forget that the purpose for which a man lives is the improvement of the man himself, so that he may go out of this world having, in his great sphere or his small one, done some little good for his fellow creatures and labored a little to diminish the sin and sorrow that are in the world.
— WILLIAM E. GLADSTONE

The ultimate value of life depends upon awareness and the power of contemplation rather than upon mere survival.
— ARISTOTLE

What saves a man is to take a step. Then another step.

It is always the same step, but you have to take it.

—ANTOINE DE SAINT-EXUPÉRY

Don't take life too seriously. You'll never get out of it alive.

—L. RON HUBBARD

Each life is made up of mistakes and learning, waiting and

growing, practicing patience and being persistent.

—BILLY GRAHAM

Each person must live their life as a model for others.

—ROSA PARKS

My philosophy of life is that if we make up our mind what we are going to make of our lives, then work hard toward that goal, we never lose—somehow we win out.
—RONALD REAGAN

Life is about making an impact, not making an income.
—KEVIN KRUSE

Love your enemies, for they tell you your faults.
—BENJAMIN FRANKLIN

Enjoy when you can, and endure when you must.
—JOHANN WOLFGANG VON GOETHE

The biggest adventure you can take is to live the life of your dreams.
—OPRAH WINFREY

•

The two most important days in your life are the day
you are born and the day you find out why.
—MARK TWAIN

•

The most difficult thing is the decision to act,
the rest is merely tenacity.
—AMELIA EARHART

•

O, what a tangled web we weave / when first we practice to deceive!
—SIR WALTER SCOTT

The greatest day in your life and mine is when we take total
responsibility for our attitudes. That's the day we truly grow up.
—JOHN C. MAXWELL

Never miss an opportunity to make others happy,
even if you have to leave them alone in order to do it.
—SOURCE UNKNOWN

Do not confuse your vested interests with ethics. Do not identify
the enemies of your privilege with the enemies of humanity.
—MAX LERNER

Life is ten percent what happens to you and

ninety percent how you respond to it.

—LOU HOLTZ

•

See everything; overlook a great deal; correct a little.

—POPE JOHN XXIII

•

Believe that life is worth living and your belief will help create the fact.

—WILLIAM JAMES

•

The only disability in life is a bad attitude.

—SCOTT HAMILTON

Have courage for the great sorrows of life and patience
for the small ones; and when you have laboriously
accomplished your daily task, go to sleep in peace.
—VICTOR HUGO

We have to live today by what truth we can get today
and be ready tomorrow to call it falsehood.
—WILLIAM JAMES

Too often we underestimate the power of a touch, a smile, a kind
word, a listening ear, an honest compliment, or the smallest act
of caring, all of which have the potential to turn a life around.
—LEO BUSCAGLIA

Life isn't about finding yourself. Life is about creating yourself.
—GEORGE BERNARD SHAW

Tomorrow is the most important thing in life. Comes into us at midnight very clean. It's perfect when it arrives and it puts itself in our hands. It hopes we've learnt something from yesterday.
—INSCRIPTION ON JOHN WAYNE'S HEADSTONE

You are as young as your faith, as old as your doubt;
as young as your self-confidence, as old as your fear;
as young as your hope, as old as your despair.
—DOUGLAS MACARTHUR

I make the most of all that comes and the least of all that goes.

—SARA TEASDALE

•

There is no passion to be found playing small—in settling for

a life that is less than the one you are capable of living.

—NELSON MANDELA

•

Every ten years a man should give himself a good kick in the pants.

—EDWARD STEICHEN

•

Life is not a problem to be solved, but a reality to be experienced.

—SØREN KIERKEGAARD

Whatever you can do, or dream you can, begin it.

Boldness has genius, power and magic in it.
—JOHANN WOLFGANG VON GOETHE

●

People grow through experience if they meet life honestly

and courageously. This is how character is built.
—ELEANOR ROOSEVELT

●

The most common way people give up their

power is by thinking they don't have any.
—ALICE WALKER

●

Character may be manifested in the great moments,

but it is made in the small ones.
—SIR WINSTON CHURCHILL

Our prime purpose in this life is to help others.
And if you can't help them, at least don't hurt them.
—DALAI LAMA

Excess on occasion is exhilarating. It prevents moderation
from acquiring the deadening effect of a habit.
—W. SOMERSET MAUGHAM

Provide yourself with friends as well as kin—
one loyal friend is worth ten thousand kinsmen.
—EURIPIDES

Don't be afraid of death so much as an inadequate life.
—BERTOLT BRECHT

If you always do what you have done,

you will always get what you have got.

—SOURCE UNKNOWN

●

Half the failures in life arise from pulling in the horse as he is leaping.

—AUGUSTUS WILLIAM HARE AND JULIUS CHARLES HARE

●

Look at everything as though you were seeing

it either for the first or last time.

—BETTY SMITH

A strange thing is memory, and hope; one looks backward, and the other forward; one is of today, the other of tomorrow. Memory is history recorded in our brain, memory is a painter, it paints pictures of the past and of the day.
—ANNA MARY ROBERTSON ("GRANDMA") MOSES

We are cups, constantly and quietly being filled. The trick is, knowing how to tip ourselves over and let the beautiful stuff out.
—RAY BRADBURY

Conscience is a man's compass, and though the needle sometimes deviates, though one often perceives irregularities when directing one's course by it, one must still try to follow its direction.
—VINCENT VAN GOGH

There is no such thing in anyone's life as an unimportant day.
—**ALEXANDER WOOLLCOTT**

•

Want of care does us more damage than want of knowledge.
—**BENJAMIN FRANKLIN**

•

It is every man's obligation to put back into the world
at least the equivalent of what he takes out of it.
—**ALBERT EINSTEIN**

If only I may grow: firmer, simpler, quieter, warmer.

—DAG HAMMARSKJÖLD

•

Keep trying, hold on, and always, always, always believe in yourself,
because if you don't, then who will, sweetie? So keep your head
high, keep your chin up, and most importantly, keep smiling,
because life's a beautiful thing and there's so much to smile about.

—MARILYN MONROE

•

Try to be a rainbow in someone's cloud.

—MAYA ANGELOU

Most of the shadows of this life are caused by

our standing in our own sunshine.

—RALPH WALDO EMERSON

•

Don't judge each day by the harvest you reap

but by the seeds that you plant.

—ROBERT LOUIS STEVENSON

•

In this age, which believes that there is a short cut to

everything, the greatest lesson to be learned is that the

most difficult way is, in the long run, the easiest.

—HENRY MILLER

In the hopes of reaching the moon men fail to
see the flowers that blossom at their feet.
— **ALBERT SCHWEITZER**

•

Live a good, honorable life. Then when you get older
and think back, you'll enjoy it a second time.
— **SOURCE UNKNOWN**

•

The pessimist complains about the wind; the optimist
expects it to change; the realist adjusts the sails.
— **WILLIAM ARTHUR WARD**

•

Don't ever take a fence down until you know why it was put up.
— **ROBERT FROST**

Whatever you are, try to be a good one.
—WILLIAM MAKEPEACE THACKERAY

The day will happen whether or not you get up.
—JOHN CIARDI

Never miss a good chance to shut up.
—WILL ROGERS

Work is the best antidote to sorrow, my dear Watson.
—SIR ARTHUR CONAN DOYLE

To finish the moment, to find the journey's end in every step of the road, to live the greatest number of good hours, is wisdom.
—RALPH WALDO EMERSON

None are so old as those who have outlived enthusiasm.
—HENRY DAVID THOREAU

Life's most persistent and urgent question is,
"What are you doing for others?"
—MARTIN LUTHER KING JR.

Life is a series of natural and spontaneous changes. Don't resist
them—that only creates sorrow. Let reality be reality. Let
things flow naturally forward in whatever way they like.
—LAO-TZU

Change is the law of life. And those who look only to
the past or present are certain to miss the future.
—JOHN F. KENNEDY

Never let your sense of morals prevent you from doing what is right.
—ISAAC ASIMOV

Never ruin an apology with an excuse.
—BENJAMIN FRANKLIN

The longer I live the more beautiful life becomes. If you
foolishly ignore beauty, you will soon find yourself without
it. Your life will be impoverished. But if you invest in
beauty, it will remain with you all the days of your life.
—FRANK LLOYD WRIGHT

You've got to work with your mistakes until they look intended.
—RAYMOND CARVER

A society grows great when old men plant trees whose
shade they know they shall never sit in.
—ARISTOTLE

There is a time for departure even when there's no certain place to go.

—TENNESSEE WILLIAMS

•

"I'm bored" is a useless thing to say. I mean, you live in a great, big, vast world that you've seen none percent of. Even the inside of your own mind is endless; it goes on forever, inwardly, do you understand? The fact that you're alive is amazing, so you don't get to say "I'm bored."

—LOUIS C.K.

•

At age 20, we worry about what others think of us.

At age 40, we don't care what they think of us.

At age 60, we discover they haven't been thinking of us at all.

—ANN LANDERS

If I can stop one heart from breaking,

I shall not live in vain.

If I can ease one life the aching,

Or cool one pain,

Or help one fainting robin

Unto his nest again,

I shall not live in vain.

—EMILY DICKINSON

II.

Love
and
Friendship

What is a friend? A single soul dwelling in two bodies.
—ARISTOTLE

Always be a little kinder than necessary.
—SIR JAMES MATTHEW BARRIE

People are unreasonable, illogical, and self-centered. Love them anyway.
—MOTHER TERESA

To err is human, to forgive divine.
—ALEXANDER POPE

To err is human; to forgive, infrequent.
—FRANKLIN P. ADAMS

A person is only as good as what they love.
—SAUL BELLOW

And in the end, the love you take is equal to the love you make.
— PAUL MCCARTNEY

•

To give counsel as well as to take it is a feature of true friendship.
— MARCUS TULLIUS CICERO

•

Thousands of candles can be lighted from a single
candle, And the life of the candle will not be shortened.
Happiness never decreases by being shared.
— BUDDHA

•

Kind hearts are more than coronets /
And simple faith than Norman blood.
— ALFRED, LORD TENNYSON

Laughter is the closest distance between two people.
—**VICTOR BORGE**

A heart can be broken, but it will keep beating just the same.
—**FANNIE FLAGG**

Love is like war; easy to begin but very hard to stop.
—**H. L. MENCKEN**

It is well, when judging a friend, to remember that he is judging

you with the same godlike and superior impartiality.
—**ARNOLD BENNETT**

Though you break your heart, men will go on as before.
—MARCUS AURELIUS

•

I count myself in nothing else so happy /

As in a soul rememb'ring my good friends.
—WILLIAM SHAKESPEARE

•

The heart has its reasons of which reason knows nothing.
—BLAISE PASCAL

•

Have a heart that never hardens, a temper that

never tires, a touch that never hurts.
—CHARLES DICKENS

To give pleasure to a single heart by a single kind act is
better than a thousand head-bowings in prayer.
—SAADI

Goodness does not consist in greatness, but greatness in goodness.
—ATHENAEUS

How should we like it / were stars to burn /
With a passion for us we / could not return /
If equal affection there cannot be /
Let the more loving one be me.
—W. H. AUDEN

Love is a great beautifier.
—LOUISA MAY ALCOTT

Few men have the natural strength to honour
a friend's success without envy.
—AESCHYLUS

There might be some credit in being jolly.
—CHARLES DICKENS

Kind words do not cost much. They never blister the tongue or
lips. They make other people good-natured. They also produce
their own image on men's souls, and a beautiful image it is.
—BLAISE PASCAL

If you have only one smile in you, give it to the people
you love. Don't be surly at home, then go out in the street
and start grinning "Good morning" at total strangers.
— **MAYA ANGELOU**

Without friends no one would choose to live,
though he had all other goods.
— **ARISTOTLE**

An insincere and evil friend is more to be feared
than a wild beast; a wild beast may wound your body,
but an evil friend will wound your mind.
— **BUDDHA**

It is a good thing to be rich and a good thing to be strong,

but it is a better thing to be loved by many friends.

—EURIPIDES

It's sad when someone you know becomes someone you knew.

—HENRY ROLLINS

Your friends will know you better in the first moment you

meet than your acquaintances will know you in a lifetime.

—RICHARD BACH

It is in pardoning that we are pardoned.

—SAINT FRANCIS OF ASSISI

In those whom I like, I can find no common denominator;
in those whom I love I can: they all make me laugh.
— W. H. AUDEN

Those who bring sunshine to the lives of others
cannot keep it from themselves.
— SIR JAMES MATTHEW BARRIE

The person who tries to live alone will not succeed as a
human being. His heart withers if it does not answer another
heart. His mind shrinks away if he hears only the echoes
of his own thoughts and finds no other inspiration.
— PEARL S. BUCK

One of the surest evidences of friendship that one
individual can display to another is telling him gently of
a fault. If any other can excel it, it is listening to such a
disclosure with gratitude, and amending the error.
—EDWARD GEORGE BULWER-LYTTON

Don't smother each other. No one can grow in the shade.
—LEO BUSCAGLIA

I always felt that the great high privilege, relief and comfort
of friendship was that one had to explain nothing.
—KATHERINE MANSFIELD

Friendship is like money, easier made than kept.
—SAMUEL BUTLER

You are forgiven for your happiness and your successes
only if you generously consent to share them.
—**ALBERT CAMUS**

Love is an irresistible desire to be irresistibly desired.
—**ROBERT FROST**

If you want to win friends, make it a point to remember them.
If you remember my name, you pay me a subtle compliment;
you indicate that I have made an impression on you. Remember
my name and you add to my feeling of importance.
—**DALE CARNEGIE**

If you would stand well with a great mind, leave him with
a favorable impression of yourself; if with a little mind,
leave him with a favorable impression of himself.
—SAMUEL TAYLOR COLERIDGE

You shall judge a man by his foes as well as by his friends.
—JOSEPH CONRAD

As old wood is best to burn; old horses to ride;
old books to read; old wine to drink;
so are old friends most trusty to use.
—LEONARD WRIGHT

Advice from your friends is like the weather,

some of it is good, some of it is bad.

—ANONYMOUS

A friend is a person with whom I may be sincere.

Before him, I may think aloud.

—RALPH WALDO EMERSON

A loving heart is the truest wisdom.

—CHARLES DICKENS

The glory of friendship is not the outstretched hand, nor the kindly smile, nor the joy of companionship; it is the spiritual inspiration that comes to one when you discover that someone else believes in you and is willing to trust you with a friendship.
—RALPH WALDO EMERSON

One is very crazy when in love.
—SIGMUND FREUD

Love in its essence is spiritual fire.
—EMANUEL SWEDENBORG

Love is a hole in the heart.
—BEN HECHT

Ah, when to the heart of man / Was it ever less than a treason /
To go with the drift of things / To yield with a grace to reason /
And bow and accept at the end / Of a love or a season.

—ROBERT FROST

•

Fill each other's cup but drink not from one cup.
Give one another of your bread but eat not from the same loaf.
Sing and dance together and be joyous,
but let each one of you be alone,
Even as the strings of a lute are alone though
they quiver with the same music.

—KAHLIL GIBRAN

•

A true friend is the greatest of all blessings, and that
which we take the least care of all to acquire.

—FRANÇOIS DE LA ROCHEFOUCAULD

Friendship is born at that moment when one person says to another: What! You, too? I thought I was the only one.
—C. S. LEWIS

We must develop and maintain the capacity to forgive. He who is devoid of the power to forgive is devoid of the power to love. There is some good in the worst of us and some evil in the best of us.
—MARTIN LUTHER KING JR.

Love is a canvas furnished by Nature and embroidered by imagination.
—VOLTAIRE

We don't love qualities, we love persons; sometimes by reason of their defects as well as of their qualities.
—JACQUES MARITAIN

The most I can do for my friend is simply to be his friend.
—HENRY DAVID THOREAU

Listening is a magnetic and strange thing, a creative force.
The friends who listen to us are the ones we move toward.
When we are listened to, it creates us, makes us unfold and expand.
—DR. KARL AUGUSTUS MENNINGER

Faults shared are as comfortable as bedroom
slippers and as easy to slip into.
—PHYLLIS MCGINLEY

I have learned that to be with those I like is enough.
—WALT WHITMAN

Hold a true friend with both your hands.
—FRIEDRICH WILHELM NIETZSCHE

Absence is to love what wind is to fire; it extinguishes
the small, it enkindles the great.
—COMTE ROGER DE BUSSY-RABUTIN

A kiss is a rosy dot over the "i" of loving.
—CYRANO DE BERGERAC

Immature love says: "I love you because I need you."
Mature love says "I need you because I love you."
—ERICH FROMM

True friendship is like sound health;

the value of it is seldom known until it be lost.

— **CHARLES CALEB COLTON**

A real friend is one who walks in when the rest of the world walks out.

— **ANONYMOUS**

Don't walk in front of me, I may not follow.

Don't walk behind me, I may not lead.

Walk beside me and be my friend.

— **ALBERT CAMUS**

The deepest principle in human nature is the craving to be appreciated.

— **WILLIAM JAMES**

Forget injuries, never forget kindnesses.
—CONFUCIUS

Kindness is more important than wisdom, and the
recognition of this is the beginning of wisdom.
—THEODORE ISAAC RUBIN

Tell me who your friends are, and I will tell you who you are.
—RUSSIAN PROVERB

Let me not to the marriage of true minds
Admit impediments. Love is not love
Which alters when it alteration finds,
Or bends with the remover to remove.
O, no! It is an ever-fixed mark
That looks on tempests and is never shaken;
It is the star to every wand'ring bark,
Whose worth's unknown, although his height be taken.
Love's not Time's fool, though rosy lips and cheeks
Within his ending sickle's compass come;
Love alters not with his brief hours and weeks,
But bears it out even to the edge of doom.
If this be error and upon me proved,
I never writ, nor no man ever loved.
 — WILLIAM SHAKESPEARE

Familiar acts are beautiful through love.
—PERCY BYSSHE SHELLEY

No man is wise enough by himself.
—PLAUTUS

A friend is a present you give yourself.
—ROBERT LOUIS STEVENSON

A friend is someone who can sing you the song
of your heart when you've forgotten it.
—ANONYMOUS

The greatest good you can do for another is not just to
share your riches but to reveal to him his own.
—BENJAMIN DISRAELI

Tis better to have loved and lost / Than never to have loved at all.
—ALFRED, LORD TENNYSON

We cannot all do great things,
but we can do small things with great love.
—MOTHER TERESA

To love and win is the best thing. To love and lose, the next best.
—WILLIAM MAKEPEACE THACKERAY

My friend is one who takes me for what I am.

—HENRY DAVID THOREAU

•

Life is a flower of which love is the honey.

—VICTOR HUGO

•

You open your heart knowing that there's a chance it may be broken one day and in opening your heart, you experience a love and joy that you never dreamed possible. You find that being vulnerable is the only way to allow your heart to feel true pleasure that's so real it scares you.

—BOB MARLEY

There's beggary in the love that can be reckoned.
— **WILLIAM SHAKESPEARE**

Friends are lost by calling too often and by not calling often enough.
— **FRENCH PROVERB**

Whatever our souls are made of, his and mine are the same.
— **EMILY BRONTË**

Love doesn't sit there like a stone, it has to be made,
like bread: re-made everyday, made new.
— **URSULA K. LE GUIN**

The greatest weakness of most humans is their hesitancy to tell

others how much they love them while they're still alive.

—ORLANDO BATTISTA

Blessed is the influence of one true, loving human soul on another.

—GEORGE ELIOT

The sweetest grapes are picked from the vineyard of friendship.

—FRENCH PROVERB

No one has ever measured (not even poets)

how much love the heart can hold.

—ZELDA FITZGERALD

Love cures people, both the ones who give
it and the ones who receive it.
—DR. KARL AUGUSTUS MENNINGER

Love looks not with the eyes, but with the mind,
And therefore is winged Cupid painted blind.
—WILLIAM SHAKESPEARE

The law of love could be best understood and
learned through little children.
—MOHANDAS GANDHI

A man is only as good as what he loves.
—SAUL BELLOW

Love is a fire. But whether it is going to warm your heart
or burn down your house, you can never tell.
—**JOAN CRAWFORD**

•

I like not only to be loved, but to be told that I am loved.
—**GEORGE ELIOT**

•

Folks, I'm telling you, birthing is hard and dying is mean—
so get yourself a little loving in between.
—**LANGSTON HUGHES**

•

Everything that lives, lives not alone, not for itself.
—**WILLIAM BLAKE**

Lovers alone wear sunlight.

—E. E. CUMMINGS

Love is invisible and comes and goes where it
wants, without anyone asking about it.

—MIGUEL DE CERVANTES

The only business of the head in the world is to
bow a ceaseless obedience to the heart.

—WILLIAM BUTLER YEATS

To live without loving is to not really live.

—MOLIÈRE

Nothing changes your opinion of a friend

so surely as success—yours or his.

—**FRANKLIN P. JONES**

Am I not destroying my enemies when I make friends of them?

—**ABRAHAM LINCOLN**

The sight of lovers feedeth those in love.

—**WILLIAM SHAKESPEARE**

When I fit my thoughts to love,

even the moist-faced moon sojourns at my sleeve.

—SAIGYŌ HŌSHI

Love resembles a tree: it bends under its own weight, deeply rooted

in our being and sometimes turns green in the ruins of a heart.

—VICTOR HUGO

Two hearts in love need no words.

—MARCELINE DESBORDES-VALMORE

The measure of love is to love without measuring.
—SAINT AUGUSTINE

•

Love is a canvas furnished by Nature and embroidered by imagination.
—VOLTAIRE

III.

Success and Ways to Achieve It

Success is the ability to go from one failure to

another with no loss of enthusiasm.

—SIR WINSTON CHURCHILL

•

The obstacle is the path.

—ZEN PROVERB

•

You have brains in your head.

You have feet in your shoes.

You can steer yourself

any direction you choose.

You're on your own. And you know what you know.

And YOU are the guy who'll decide where to go.

—DR. SEUSS (THEODOR GEISEL)

Genius is one percent inspiration and ninety-nine percent perspiration.
— THOMAS ALVA EDISON

It is not enough to be busy. . . .
The question is: what are we busy about?
— HENRY DAVID THOREAU

The indispensable first step to getting the things you
want out of life is this: Decide what you want.
— BEN STEIN

All good things which exist are the fruits of originality.
— JOHN STUART MILL

The person who makes a success of living is the one who
sees his goal steadily and aims for it unswervingly.
—CECIL B. DEMILLE

The best way to make your dreams come true is to wake up.
—PAUL VALÉRY

In the field of observation, chance favors the prepared mind.
—LOUIS PASTEUR

The future belongs to those who believe in the beauty of their dreams.
—ELEANOR ROOSEVELT

Things turn out best for the people who make

the best of the way things turn out.

—JOHN R. WOODEN

Any activity becomes creative when the doer

cares about doing it right, or better.

—JOHN UPDIKE

Eighty percent of success is just showing up.

—WOODY ALLEN

Be wiser than other people, if you can; but do not tell them so.

—PHILIP DORMER STANHOPE, LORD CHESTERFIELD

No illusion is more crucial than the illusion that great success and huge money buy you immunity from the common ills of mankind, such as cars that won't start.
—LARRY MCMURTRY

When in doubt, win the trick.
—EDMOND HOYLE

There is only one boss: the customer. And he can fire everybody in the company, from the chairman on down, simply by spending his money somewhere else.
—SAM WALTON

If it be now, 'tis not to come; if it be not to come, it will be now; if it be not now, yet it will come: the readiness is all.
—WILLIAM SHAKESPEARE

The secret of successful managing is to keep the five guys who hate

you away from the four guys who haven't made up their minds.

—CHARLES "CASEY" STENGEL

Measure twice, cut once.

—CRAFTSMAN'S APHORISM

Take calculated risks. That is quite different from being rash.

—GEORGE SMITH PATTON JR.

In reading the lives of great men, I found that the first victory they

won was over themselves . . . self-discipline with all of them came first.

—HARRY S. TRUMAN

Never think that you're not good enough yourself. A man should never think that. People will take you very much at your own reckoning.
— ANTHONY TROLLOPE

It is necessary for us to learn from others' mistakes.
You will not live long enough to make them all yourself.
— HYMAN GEORGE RICKOVER

A wise man sees as much as he ought, not as much as he can.
— MICHEL DE MONTAIGNE

Without leaps of imagination, or dreaming, we lose the excitement of possibilities. Dreaming, after all, is a form of planning.
— GLORIA STEINEM

The man who trims himself to suit everybody
will soon whittle himself away.
—**CHARLES SCHWAB**

The dreadful burden of having nothing to do.
—**NICOLAS BOILEAU**

Some people believe that holding on and hanging in there are
signs of great strength. However, there are times when it takes
much more strength to know when to let go—and then do it.
—**ANN LANDERS**

The greater danger for most of us lies not in setting
our aim too high and falling short, but in setting
our aim too low, and achieving our mark.
—MICHELANGELO

The cure for boredom is curiosity. There is no cure for curiosity.
—ELLEN PARR

With self-discipline most anything is possible.
—THEODORE ROOSEVELT

I always tried to turn every disaster into an opportunity.
—JOHN D. ROCKEFELLER JR.

He who does not risk will never drink champagne.
— **RUSSIAN PROVERB**

Ability is sexless.
— **JOHN HENRY NEWMAN**

For most of history, Anonymous was a woman.
— **VIRGINIA WOOLF**

Fortune favors the brave.
— **TERENCE**

I'm a great believer in luck, and I find the
harder I work the more I have of it.
—THOMAS JEFFERSON

●

One of the advantages of being disorderly is that one
is constantly making exciting discoveries.
—A. A. MILNE

●

The bravest are surely those who have the clearest
vision of what is before them, glory and danger alike,
and yet notwithstanding go out to meet it.
—THUCYDIDES

Never let your head hang down. Never give up and sit down and grieve. Find another way. And don't pray when it rains if you don't pray when the sun shines.

—**SATCHEL PAIGE**

•

You'll always miss 100% of the shots you don't take.

—**WAYNE GRETZKY**

•

There is hardly anything in the world that some man can't make a little worse and sell a little cheaper, and the people who consider price only are this man's lawful prey.

—**JOHN RUSKIN**

•

Oh, the tangled webs we weave / When we practice to deceive.

—**SIR WALTER SCOTT**

Nothing is a waste of time if you use the experience wisely.
—AUGUSTE RODIN

•

What lies behind us and what lies before us are tiny
matters compared to what lies within us.
—RALPH WALDO EMERSON

•

Work expands to fill the time available for its completion.
—CYRIL NORTHCOTE PARKINSON
(known as Parkinson's Law)

If anything can go wrong, it will.

—MURPHY'S LAW

(named after Air Force Captain Edward A. Murphy, an engineer working on a
project to see how much sudden deceleration a human can stand in a crash)

I have not failed. I've just found 10,000 ways that won't work.

—THOMAS ALVA EDISON

Formula for success: Underpromise and overdeliver.

—THOMAS PETERS

The best way to escape from a problem is to solve it.

—ANONYMOUS

A creative man is motivated by the desire to
achieve, not by the desire to beat others.
—AYN RAND

Know from whence you came. If you know whence you came,
there are absolutely no limitations to where you can go.
—JAMES BALDWIN

There is no disinfectant like success.
—DANIEL J. BOORSTIN

Nothing succeeds like success.
—ALEXANDRE DUMAS

What is harder than rock, or softer than water? Yet
soft water hollows out hard rock. Persevere.

—OVID

Prosperity is a great teacher; adversity a greater.

—WILLIAM HAZLITT

If I have seen further than others, it is by
standing upon the shoulders of giants.

—SIR ISAAC NEWTON

The spirit, the will to win, and the will to excel are
the things that endure. These qualities are so much
more important than the events that occur.

—VINCE LOMBARDI

One of the lessons of history is that nothing is often a
good thing to do and always a clever thing to say.
— **WILL DURANT**

It takes less time to do a thing right, than it
does to explain why you did it wrong.
— **HENRY WADSWORTH LONGFELLOW**

The speed of a runaway horse counts for nothing.
— **JEAN COCTEAU**

No one ever gets far unless he accomplishes
the impossible at least once a day.
— **L. RON HUBBARD**

Perfection is achieved, not when there is nothing left to
add, but when there is nothing left to take away.
—**ANTOINE DE SAINT-EXUPÉRY**

Ⓘ

It is true greatness to have in one the frailty
of a man and the security of a god.
—**LUCIUS ANNAEUS SENECA**

Ⓘ

Success is how high you bounce when you hit bottom.
—**GEORGE SMITH PATTON JR.**

Ⓘ

A bank is a place where they lend you an umbrella in fair
weather and ask for it back when it begins to rain.
—**ROBERT FROST**

We often discover what will do, by finding out what will not do; and
probably he who never made a mistake never made a discovery.
—SAMUEL SMILES

•

One thing life taught me: if you are interested, you never have to
look for new interests. They come to you. When you are genuinely
interested in one thing, it will always lead to something else.
—ELEANOR ROOSEVELT

•

To do good things in the world, first you must know
who you are and what gives meaning to your life.
—ROBERT BROWNING

You just don't luck into things as much as you'd like to think you do.
You build step by step, whether it's friendships or opportunities.
—**BARBARA BUSH**

Whether you think you can or whether you
think you can't, you're right.
—**HENRY FORD**

An inconvenience is only an adventure wrongly considered;
an adventure is an inconvenience rightly considered.
—**G. K. CHESTERTON**

It is the part of a wise man to keep himself to-day for tomorrow, and not to venture all his eggs in one basket.
—**MIGUEL DE CERVANTES**

To please everybody is impossible; were I to undertake
it, I should probably please nobody.
—**GEORGE WASHINGTON**

•

During my eighty-seven years I have witnessed a whole succession
of technological revolutions. But none of them has done away with
the need for character in the individual or the ability to think.
—**BERNARD MANNES BARUCH**

•

When clouds form in the skies we know that rain will follow but
we must not wait for it. Nothing will be achieved by attempting to
interfere with the future before the time is ripe. Patience is needed.
—**I CHING**

Keep away from people who try to belittle your ambitions.
Small people always do that, but the really great
make you feel that you too, can become great.
—MARK TWAIN

A good solution applied with vigor now is better than
a perfect solution applied ten minutes later.
—GEORGE SMITH PATTON JR.

Being a hero is about the shortest-lived profession on earth.
—WILL ROGERS

One day Alice came to a fork in the road and saw
a Cheshire cat in a tree. "Which road do I take?" she asked.
"Where do you want to go?" was his response. "I don't know,"
Alice answered. "Then," said the cat, "it doesn't matter."
—LEWIS CARROLL

Spoon feeding in the long run teaches us

nothing but the shape of the spoon.

—E. M. FORSTER

•

If I have ever made any valuable discoveries, it has been

owing more to patient attention, than to any other talent.

—SIR ISAAC NEWTON

•

If a man will begin with certainties, he shall end in doubts; but if he

will be content to begin with doubts, he shall end in certainties.

—SIR FRANCIS BACON

•

I not only use all the brains that I have, but all that I can borrow.

—WOODROW WILSON

They say that time changes things,

but you actually have to change them yourself.

—ANDY WARHOL

•

It is a paradoxical but profoundly true and important principle of

life that the most likely way to reach a goal is to be aiming not

at that goal itself but at some more ambitious goal beyond it.

—ARNOLD JOSEPH TOYNBEE

•

It is a bad plan that admits of no modification.

—PUBLILIUS SYRUS

•

It takes as much energy to wish as it does to plan.

—ELEANOR ROOSEVELT

One of the annoying things about believing in free will and individual responsibility is the difficulty of finding somebody to blame your problems on. And when you do find somebody, it's remarkable how often his picture turns up on your driver's license.

—P. J. O'ROURKE

Who dares, wins.

—ANONYMOUS

It does not matter how slowly you go so long as you do not stop.

—CONFUCIUS

I learned much from my teachers, more from my books, and most from my mistakes.

—ANONYMOUS

A wise man will make more opportunities than he finds.

—SIR FRANCIS BACON

If the only tool you have is a hammer, every problem looks like a nail.

—ABRAHAM MASLOW

Next to knowing when to seize an opportunity,
the next important thing is to know when to forego an advantage.

—BENJAMIN DISRAELI

Lead, follow, or get out of the way.

—THOMAS PAINE

The manner in which a man chooses to gamble
indicates his character or his lack of it.
—WILLIAM SAROYAN

•

If you wish in this world to advance,
Your merits you're bound to enhance;
You must stir it and stump it,
and blow your own trumpet.
Or trust me, you haven't a chance.
—SIR WILLIAM S. GILBERT

•

Leadership is solving problems. The day soldiers stop bringing
you their problems is the day you have stopped leading them.
They have either lost confidence that you can help or concluded
you do not care. Either case is a failure of leadership.
—COLIN POWELL

You can't always get what you want /

But if you try sometime you might find /

You get what you need.

—**MICK JAGGER AND KEITH RICHARDS**

Success is dependent on effort.

—**SOPHOCLES**

People cannot be managed. Inventories can

be managed, but people must be led.

—**H. ROSS PEROT**

If you believe you can, you probably can. If you believe

you won't, you most assuredly won't. Belief is the ignition

switch that gets you off the launching pad.

—**DENIS WAITLEY**

It doesn't matter if a cat is black or white, so long as it catches mice.
—DENG XIAOPING

•

A good objective of leadership is to help those who are doing poorly
to do well and to help those who are doing well to do even better.
—JIM ROHN

•

Clear your mind of can't.
—SOLON

•

Giving your son a skill is better than giving
him one thousand pieces of gold.
—CHINESE PROVERB

. . . Give every man thy ear, but few thy voice;

Take each man's censure, but reserve thy judgment.

Costly thy habit as thy purse can buy . . .

Neither a borrower nor a lender be;

For loan oft loses both itself and friend,

And borrowing dulls the edge of husbandry.

— **WILLIAM SHAKESPEARE**

There is no such thing as a "self-made" person. . . . Everyone who has ever done a kind deed for us, or spoken one word of encouragement to us, has entered into the make-up of our character and of our thoughts, as well as our success.

— **GEORGE MATTHEW ADAMS**

Difficulty, my brethren, is the nurse of greatness—a harsh nurse, who roughly rocks her foster-children into strength and athletic proportion.

— **WILLIAM CULLEN BRYANT**

If nothing ever changed, there'd be no butterflies.
—ANONYMOUS

•

Progress, far from consisting in change, depends on retentiveness. When change is absolute there remains no being to improve and no direction is set for possible improvement: and when experience is not retained, as among savages, infancy is perpetual. Those who cannot remember the past are condemned to repeat it.
—GEORGE SANTAYANA

•

The man who has no imagination has no wings.
—MUHAMMAD ALI

•

I love the man that can smile in trouble, that can gather strength from distress, and grow brave by reflection. 'Tis the business of little minds to shrink, but he whose heart is firm, and whose conscience approves his conduct, will pursue his principles unto death.
—THOMAS PAINE

I try to do the right thing at the right time.

They may just be little things, but usually they make

the difference between winning and losing.

—**KAREEM ABDUL-JABBAR**

•

Great deeds are usually wrought at great risks.

—**HERODOTUS**

•

Prosperity depends more on wanting what you

have than having what you want.

—**GEOFFREY F. ABERT**

•

If it sounds too good to be true, it is.

—**ANONYMOUS**

Never esteem anything as of advantage to you that will
make you break your word or lose your self-respect.
—HENRY BROOKS ADAMS

If you're not failing every now and again, it's a sign
you're not doing anything very innovative.
—WOODY ALLEN

If you don't like something, change it. If you can't
change it, change your attitude. Don't complain.
—MAYA ANGELOU

We are what we repeatedly do, excellence is
therefore not an act but a habit.
—ARISTOTLE

Never play cards with a man called Doc, never eat at a place called Mom's, and never sleep with a woman whose troubles are worse than your own.
—NELSON ALGREN

Less is more.
—LUDWIG MIES VAN DER ROHE

All things are difficult before they are easy.
—THOMAS FULLER

It is not always by plugging away at a difficulty and sticking at it that one overcomes it; but, rather, often by working on the one next to it. Certain people and certain things require to be approached on an angle.
—MATTHEW ARNOLD

A subtle thought that is in error may yet give rise to fruitful inquiry that can establish truths of great value.

—ISAAC ASIMOV

If money be not thy servant, it will be thy master. The covetous man cannot so properly be said to possess wealth, as that may be said to possess him.

—SIR FRANCIS BACON

One of the things I learned the hard way was that it doesn't pay to get discouraged. Keeping busy and making optimism a way of life can restore your faith in yourself.

—LUCILLE BALL

In a hierarchy every employee tends to rise to his level of incompetence.

—LAURENCE J. PETER
(expressing the so-called Peter Principle)

Those who know how to win are more numerous than those who know how to make proper use of their victories.

— POLYBIUS

Power is not revealed by striking hard or often, but by striking true.

— HONORÉ DE BALZAC

Millions saw the apple fall, but Newton was the one who asked why.

— BERNARD MANNES BARUCH

It's what you learn after you know it all that's important.

— JIMMY WILLIAMS

Call it what you will, incentives are what get people to work harder.
— **NIKITA KHRUSHCHEV**

•

What makes a good follower? The single most important characteristic may well be a willingness to tell the truth. In a world of growing complexity leaders are increasingly dependent on their subordinates for good information, whether the leaders want to hear it or not. Followers who tell the truth and leaders who listen to it are an unbeatable combination.
— **WARREN G. BENNIS**

•

Riches do not consist in the possession of treasures, but in the use made of them.
— **NAPOLÉON BONAPARTE**

The best computer is a man, and it's the only one
that can be mass-produced by unskilled labor.
—WERNHER VON BRAUN

A hunch is creativity trying to tell you something.
—FRANK CAPRA

Any fool can make things bigger, more complex, and
more violent. It takes a touch of genius—and a lot of
courage—to move in the opposite direction.
—ALBERT EINSTEIN

The person interested in success has to learn to view failure as a
healthy, inevitable part of the process of getting to the top.
—DR. JOYCE BROTHERS

Good judgment comes from experience, and
experience usually comes from bad judgment.
— ANONYMOUS

Ah, but a man's reach should exceed his grasp—or what's a heaven for?
— ROBERT BROWNING

The way to develop self-confidence is to do the thing you
fear and get a record of successful experiences behind you.
Destiny is not a matter of chance, it is a matter of choice; it is
not a thing to be waited for, it is a thing to be achieved.
— WILLIAM JENNINGS BRYAN

Believe nothing merely because you have been told it. Do not believe
what your teacher tells you merely out of respect for the teacher.
But whatsoever, after due examination and analysis, you find to be
kind, conducive to the good, the benefit, the welfare of all beings—
that doctrine believe and cling to, and take it as your guide.
— BUDDHA

You can do very little with faith, but you can do nothing without it.
—SAMUEL BUTLER

When you follow your bliss . . . doors will open where
you would not have thought there would be doors; and
where there wouldn't be a door for anyone else.
—JOSEPH CAMPBELL

The truth that many people never understand, until it is too
late, is that the more you try to avoid suffering the more you
suffer because smaller and more insignificant things begin
to torture you in proportion to your fear of being hurt.
—THOMAS MERTON

You can get a lot farther with a kind word
and a gun than a kind word alone.
—AL CAPONE

The man without a purpose is like a ship without a rudder—a waif, a nothing, a no man. Have a purpose in life and having it, throw such strength of mind and muscle into your work as God has given you.

—THOMAS CARLYLE

•

"Where shall I begin, please, your Majesty?" he asked. "Begin at the beginning," the King said, gravely, "and go on till you come to the end: then stop."

—LEWIS CARROLL

•

Perseverance alone does not assure success. No amount of stalking will lead to game in a field that has none.

—I CHING

•

For myself I am an optimist—it does not seem to be much use being anything else.

—SIR WINSTON CHURCHILL

Nothing in the world can take the place of persistence. Talent will not; nothing is more common than unsuccessful men with talent. Genius will not; unrewarded genius is almost a proverb. Education will not; the world is full of educated derelicts. Persistence and determination are omnipotent.

—CALVIN COOLIDGE

Iron rusts from disuse; stagnant water loses it purity and in cold weather becomes frozen; even so does inaction sap the vigor of the mind.

—LEONARDO DA VINCI

Believe those who are seeking the truth; doubt those who find it.

—ANDRÉ GIDE

The only safe thing is to take a chance. Play safe and you are dead. Taking risks is the essence of good work, and the difference between safe and bold can only be defined by yourself since no one else knows for what you are hoping when you embark on anything.

—MIKE NICHOLS

Sometimes you have to play for a long time
to be able to play like yourself.
—MILES DAVIS JR.

●

It is a common experience that a problem difficult at night is resolved
in the morning after a committee of sleep has worked on it.
—JOHN STEINBECK

●

Small opportunities are often the beginning of great enterprises.
—DEMOSTHENES

●

If you're not making mistakes, you're not trying hard enough.
—VINCE LOMBARDI

Failure is instructive. The person who really thinks learns
quite as much from his failures as from his successes.
—JOHN DEWEY

Luck is the residue of design.
—BRANCH RICKEY

Speak the truth, do not yield to anger; give, if thou art asked
for little; by these three steps thou wilt go near the gods.
—THE DHAMMAPADA

Nothing can be produced out of nothing.
—DIOGENES LAERTIUS

When you have eliminated the impossible,
that which remains, however improbable, must be the truth.
—**SIR ARTHUR CONAN DOYLE**

You can't build a reputation on what you're going to do.
—**HENRY FORD**

The winds and the waves are always on the
side of the ablest navigators.
—**EDWARD GIBBON**

Annual income twenty pounds, annual expenditure nineteen
pounds and six, result happiness. Annual income twenty pounds,
annual expenditure twenty pounds ought and six, result misery.
—**CHARLES DICKENS**

Don't accept your dog's admiration as conclusive
evidence that you are wonderful.
—ANN LANDERS

Nothing great was ever achieved without enthusiasm.
—RALPH WALDO EMERSON

The world is full of willing people; some willing
to work, the rest willing to let them.
—ROBERT FROST

I respect the man who knows distinctly what he wishes.
The greater part of all mischief in the world arises from the fact
that men do not sufficiently understand their own aims. They
have undertaken to build a tower, and spend no more labor
on the foundation than would be necessary to erect a hut.
—JOHANN WOLFGANG VON GOETHE

You cannot play with the animal in you without becoming wholly animal, play with falsehood without forfeiting your right to truth, play with cruelty without losing your sensitivity of mind. He who wants to keep his garden tidy doesn't reserve a plot for weeds.

—DAG HAMMARSKJÖLD

My weakness has always been to prefer the large intention of an unskillful artist to the trivial intention of an accomplished one: in other words, I am more interested in the high ideas of a feeble executant than in the high execution of a feeble thinker.

—THOMAS HARDY

I have the simplest tastes. I am always satisfied with the best.

—OSCAR WILDE

We are wiser than we know.

—RALPH WALDO EMERSON

Happiness is as a butterfly which, when pursued,
is always beyond our grasp, but which if you will
sit down quietly, may alight upon you.
—NATHANIEL HAWTHORNE

There is a tide in the affairs of men,
Which taken at the flood, leads on to fortune;
Omitted, all the voyage of their life
Is bound in shallows and in miseries.
—WILLIAM SHAKESPEARE

I find the great thing in this world is not so much where
we stand, as in what direction we are moving—we must
sail sometimes with the wind and sometimes against it—
but we must sail, and not drift, nor lie at anchor.
—OLIVER WENDELL HOLMES JR.

I have had dreams and I have had nightmares,

but I have conquered my nightmares because of my dreams.

—JONAS SALK

Trifles make perfections, but perfection is itself no trifle.

—SHAKER PROVERB

Experience is not what happens to you,

it is what you do with what happens to you.

—ALDOUS HUXLEY

Nothing is built on stone; all is built on sand,

but we must build as if the sand were stone.

—JORGE LUIS BORGES

A man must be big enough to admit his mistakes, smart enough
to profit from them, and strong enough to correct them.
—JOHN C. MAXWELL

•

Nothing will ever be attempted if all possible
objections must first be overcome.
—SAMUEL JOHNSON

•

There is only one success—
to be able to spend your life in your own way.
—CHRISTOPHER DARLINGTON MORLEY

•

The most pathetic person in the world is someone
who has sight, but has no vision.
—HELEN KELLER

You ain't gonna learn what you don't wanna know.

—JERRY GARCIA

•

If men could regard the events of their own lives with more open minds, they would frequently discover that they did not really desire the things they failed to obtain.

—ANDRÉ MAUROIS

•

The highest reward for a man's toil is not what he gets for it but what he becomes by it.

—JOHN RUSKIN

•

Practice doesn't make perfect. Perfect practice makes perfect.

—VINCE LOMBARDI

It takes as much stress to be a success as it does to be a failure.
—EMILIO JAMES TRUJILLO

•

In the fight between you and the world, back the world.
—FRANZ KAFKA

•

There is always an easy solution to every human problem—
neat, plausible, and wrong.
—H. L. MENCKEN

•

Imagination will often carry us to worlds that
never were. But without it we go nowhere.
—CARL SAGAN

A timid person is frightened before a danger, a coward
during the time, and a courageous person afterward.
—JEAN PAUL FRIEDRICH RICHTER

•

A habit cannot be tossed out the window;
it must be coaxed down the stairs a step at a time.
—MARK TWAIN

•

Mishaps are like knives, that either serve us or cut us,
as we grasp them by the blade or the handle.
—JAMES RUSSELL LOWELL

•

The two most powerful warriors are patience and time.
—LEO TOLSTOY

The greatest glory in living lies not in never falling,

but in rising every time we fall.

—**NELSON MANDELA**

Everybody knows if you are too careful you are so occupied in

being careful that you are sure to stumble over something.

—**GERTRUDE STEIN**

A professional is a man who can do his best at a

time when he doesn't particularly feel like it.

—**ALISTAIR COOKE**

The man who can drive himself further once the

effort gets painful is the man who will win.

—**ROGER BANNISTER**

Do continue to believe that with your feeling and your work you
are taking part in the greatest; the more strongly you cultivate
this belief, the more will reality and the world go forth from it.
—RAINER MARIA RILKE

Doing the best at this moment puts you in the
best place for the next moment.
—OPRAH WINFREY

There are no menial jobs, only menial attitudes.
—WILLIAM JOHN BENNETT

Mistakes are the portals for discovery.
—JAMES JOYCE

The pupil who is never required to do what he
cannot do, never does what he can do.
— **JOHN STUART MILL**

•

God doth not need
Either man's work or his own gifts; who best
Bear his mild yoke, they serve him best; his State
Is Kingly. Thousands at his bidding speed
And post o'er Land and Ocean without rest:
They also serve who only stand and wait.
— **JOHN MILTON**

•

Never tell people how to do things. Tell them what you want
them to achieve, and they will surprise you with their ingenuity.
— **GEORGE SMITH PATTON JR.**

There are two kinds of failures: those who thought and
never did, and those who did and never thought.
—**LAURENCE J. PETER**

•

Obstacles are those frightful things you see
when you take your eyes off your goal.
—**HENRY FORD**

•

Problems are only opportunities in work clothes.
—**HENRY J. KAISER**

•

Use what talents you possess: the woods would be very silent
if no birds sang there except those that sang best.
—**HENRY VAN DYKE**

Success usually comes to those who are too busy to be looking for it.
—HENRY DAVID THOREAU

I would rather fail in a cause that will ultimately triumph
than to triumph in cause that will ultimately fail.
—WOODROW WILSON

One should not increase, beyond what is necessary,
the number of entities required to explain anything.
—WILLIAM OF OCCAM
(This principle of parsimony is known as "Occam's razor.")

When I am working on a problem, I never think about beauty . . .
but when I have finished, if the solution is not beautiful,
I know it is wrong.
—R. BUCKMINSTER FULLER

Merely having an open mind is nothing; the object of opening the mind, as of opening the mouth, is to shut it again on something solid.
— G. K. CHESTERTON

Blessed is the man who, having nothing to say, abstains from giving us wordy evidence of the fact.
— GEORGE ELIOT

Curiosity . . . endows the people who have it with a generosity in argument and a serenity in cheerful willingness to let life take the form it will.
— ALISTAIR COOKE

Ideas won't keep; something must be done about them.
— ALFRED NORTH WHITEHEAD

When people keep telling you that you can't
do a thing, you kind of like to try it.
—MARGARET CHASE SMITH

Never grow a wishbone where your backbone ought to be.
—CLEMENTINE PADDLEFORD

Nobody can make you feel inferior without your consent.
—ELEANOR ROOSEVELT

Kind words are short and easy to speak,
but their echoes are truly endless.
—MOTHER TERESA

Commit yourself to a dream. . . . Nobody who tries to do something great but fails is a total failure. Why? Because he can always rest assured that he succeeded in life's most important battle—he defeated the fear of trying.

—ROBERT H. SCHULLER

You can be discouraged by failure—or you can learn from it. So go ahead and make mistakes. Make all you can. Because, remember that's where you'll find success—on the far side.

—THOMAS WATSON SR.

I am always doing that which I cannot do,
in order that I may learn how to do it.

—PABLO PICASSO

Always do sober what you said you'd do drunk.
That will teach you to keep your mouth shut.

—ERNEST HEMINGWAY

There is nothing more difficult to take in hand, more perilous
to conduct, or more uncertain in its success, than to take
the lead in the introduction of a new order to things.
—NICCOLÒ MACHIAVELLI

Diamonds are nothing more than chunks
of coal that stuck to their jobs.
—MALCOLM FORBES

Ambition can creep as well as soar.
—EDMUND BURKE

If we work upon marble, it will perish; if we work upon brass,
time will efface it; if we rear temples, they will crumble into dust;
but if we work upon immortal minds and instill into them just
principles, we are then engraving that upon tablets which no
time will efface, but will brighten and brighten to all eternity.
—DANIEL WEBSTER

The best leaders of all are ones the people do not know exist.

They turn to each other and say we did it ourselves.

—ZEN APHORISM

•

They can do all because they think they can.

—VIRGIL

•

White. A blank page or canvas. So many possibilities.

—STEPHEN SONDHEIM

•

We're all proud of making little mistakes.

It gives us the feeling we don't make any big ones.

— ANDREW A. "ANDY" ROONEY

People have been known to achieve more as a result
of working with others than against them.
—**DR. ALLAN FROMME**

People have been known to achieve more as a result

Four things come not back: the spoken word,
the spent arrow, the past, the neglected opportunity.
—**OMAR IBN AL-HALIF**

Anywhere is walking distance, if you've got the time.
—**STEVEN WRIGHT**

A jest's prosperity lies in the ear of him that hears it,
never in the tongue of him that makes it.
—**WILLIAM SHAKESPEARE**

Trust yourself. You know more than you think you do.
—BENJAMIN SPOCK

•

I would sooner fail than not be among the greatest.
—JOHN KEATS

•

For everything you have missed, you have gained something else.
—RALPH WALDO EMERSON

•

If you don't make a total commitment to whatever you're doing,
then you start looking to bail out the first time the boat starts leaking.
It's tough enough getting that boat to shore with everybody rowing,
let alone when a guy stands up and starts putting his jacket on.
—LOU HOLTZ

When you reach for the stars, you may not quite get them,

but you won't come up with a handful of mud either.

—LEO BURNETT

When the will defies fear, when the heart applauds the brain,

when duty throws the gauntlet down to fate, when honor

scorns to compromise with death—this is heroism.

—ROBERT INGERSOLL

Let fear be a counselor and not a jailer.

—TONY ROBBINS

Envy, among other ingredients, has a mixture of love of justice in it.

We are more angry at undeserved than at deserved good fortune.

—WILLIAM HAZLITT

Things don't change, but by and by our wishes change.
—MARCEL PROUST

Having once decided to achieve a certain task, achieve it at
all cost of tedium and distaste. The gain in self-confidence
of having accomplished a tiresome labor is immense.
—ARNOLD BENNETT

He who desires but acts not, breeds pestilence.
—WILLIAM BLAKE

The artist is nothing without the gift,
but the gift is nothing without work.
—ÉMILE ZOLA

God gave us our memories so that we might have roses in December.

—SIR JAMES MATTHEW BARRIE

•

No artist is ahead of his time. He is his time.

It is just that the others are behind the time.

—MARTHA GRAHAM

•

You can never step into the same river twice;

for new waters are always flowing on to you.

—HERACLITUS

•

A work is perfectly finished only when nothing can

be added to it and nothing taken away.

—JOSEPH JOUBERT

Silence is the true friend that never betrays.

—CONFUCIUS

How often misused words generate misleading thoughts.

—HERBERT SPENCER

Beware the fury of a patient man!

—JOHN DRYDEN

A ship in harbor is safe, but that is not what ships are built for.

—JOHN A. SHEDD

What counts is not necessarily the size of the dog in the fight—

it's the size of the fight in the dog.

—DWIGHT D. EISENHOWER

•

Be like the promontory against which the waves continually break,

but it stands firm and tames the fury of the water around it.

—MARCUS AURELIUS

•

Never mistake motion for action.

—ERNEST HEMINGWAY

•

The reward of a thing well done is to have done it.

—RALPH WALDO EMERSON

Advice is like snow; the softer it falls the longer it dwells
upon, and the deeper it sinks into the mind.
—SAMUEL TAYLOR COLERIDGE

You don't need a weather man / To know which way the wind blows.
—BOB DYLAN

You trust your mother, but you cut the cards.
—ANONYMOUS

When you reach the top, keep climbing.
—ZEN APHORISM

You can observe a lot just by watching.

—**YOGI BERRA**

•

My father [President Franklin D. Roosevelt] gave me these hints

on speech-making: be sincere . . . be brief . . . be seated.

—**JAMES ROOSEVELT**

•

You've got to take the initiative and play your game.

In a decisive set, confidence is the difference.

—**CHRIS EVERT**

•

The codfish lays ten thousand eggs, the homely hen lays one. /

The codfish never cackles to tell you what she's done. /

And so we scorn the codfish, while the humble hen we prize, /

which only goes to show you that it pays to advertise.

—**ANONYMOUS**

All human wisdom is summed up in two words—wait and hope.
—ALEXANDRE DUMAS

To laugh often and much; to win the respect of intelligent people and the affection of children; to earn the appreciation of honest critics and endure the betrayal of false friends; to appreciate beauty, to find the best in others; to leave the world a little better; whether by a healthy child, a garden patch or a redeemed social condition; to know even one life has breathed easier because you have lived. This is the meaning of success.
—RALPH WALDO EMERSON

Spectacular achievement is always preceded by unspectacular preparation.
—ROBERT H. SCHULLER

A successful man is one who can lay a firm foundation
with the bricks others have thrown at him.
— **DAVID BRINKLEY**

Remember your dreams and fight for them. You must know
what you want from life. There is just one thing that makes
your dream become impossible: the fear of failure.
— **PAULO COELHO**

Industry pays debts while despair increases them.
— **BENJAMIN FRANKLIN**

It takes an intellectual to solve a problem but a genius to prevent one.
— **ALBERT EINSTEIN**

If you are immune to boredom, there is literally
nothing you cannot accomplish.
—DAVID FOSTER WALLACE

•

The great secret of success is to go through life
as a man who never gets used up.
—ALBERT SCHWEITZER

•

Keep thy shop and thy shop will keep thee.
—BENJAMIN FRANKLIN

•

Strive not to be a success, but rather to be of value.
—ALBERT EINSTEIN

Life begets life. Energy creates energy. It is by
spending oneself that one becomes rich.
—SARAH BERNHARDT

Self-assurance is two-thirds of success.
—GAELIC PROVERB

Be not angry that you cannot make others as you wish them to be,
since you cannot make yourself as you wish to be.
—SAINT THOMAS À KEMPIS

The difference between ordinary and extraordinary is that little extra.
—JIMMY JOHNSON

It wasn't raining when Noah built the ark.
—HOWARD RUFF

Have you something to do tomorrow? Do it today.
—BENJAMIN FRANKLIN

Ever tried. Ever failed. No matter. Try again. Fail again. Fail better.
—SAMUEL BECKETT

I attribute my success to this: I never gave or took any excuse.
—FLORENCE NIGHTINGALE

Definiteness of purpose is the starting point of all achievement.
—W. CLEMENT STONE

Everyone should learn to do one thing supremely well because
he likes it, and one thing supremely well because he detests it.
—BRIGHAM YOUNG

People cannot go wrong, if you don't let them.
They cannot go right, unless you let them.
—AUGUSTUS WILLIAM HARE AND JULIUS CHARLES HARE

Diligence is the mother of good luck.
— **BENJAMIN FRANKLIN**

•

Ride on! Rough-shod if need be, smooth-shod if that will do,
but ride on! Ride on over all obstacles, and win the race!
— **CHARLES DICKENS**

•

The first and greatest victory is to conquer yourself;
to be conquered by yourself is of all things most shameful and vile.
— **PLATO**

IV.

▪ ▪ ▪ ▪ ▪ ▪ ▪ ▪ ▪ ▪

The Life of the Mind

Cogito ergo sum. (I think, therefore I am.)
—RENÉ DESCARTES

•

Nothing else in the world . . . not all the armies . . .

is so powerful as an idea whose time has come.
—VICTOR HUGO

•

We are shaped by our thoughts. We become what we think.
—BUDDHA

I'd rather learn from one bird how to sing than to
teach ten thousand stars how not to dance.
—**E. E. CUMMINGS**

•

The great instrument of moral good is the imagination.
—**PERCY BYSSHE SHELLEY**

•

To be surprised, to wonder, is to begin to understand.
—**JOSÉ ORTEGA Y GASSET**

•

Knowledge is power.
—**SIR FRANCIS BACON**

It is impossible to defeat an ignorant man in argument.
— WILLIAM G. MCADOO

•

I am the wisest man alive, for I know one thing,

and that is that I know nothing.

— SOCRATES

•

Knowledge can be conveyed, but not wisdom. It can be found,

it can be lived, it is possible to be carried by it, miracles can be

performed with it, but it cannot be expressed in words and taught.

— HERMANN HESSE

Skepticism is the chastity of the intellect, and it is shameful
to surrender it too soon or to the first comer: there is nobility
in preserving it coolly and proudly through long youth,
until at last, in the ripeness of instinct and discretion, it
can be safely exchanged for fidelity and happiness.

—GEORGE SANTAYANA

Others have been here before me, and I walk in their footsteps.
The books I have read were composed by generations of fathers
and sons, mothers and daughters, teachers and disciples. I am the
sum total of their experiences, their quests. And so are you.

—ELIE WIESEL

If we value the pursuit of knowledge, we must be free to
follow wherever that search may lead us. The free mind is
no barking dog to be tethered on a one-foot chain.
—THEODOR ADORNO

•

The test of a first-rate intelligence is the ability to hold two opposed
ideas in the mind at the same time, and still retain the ability
to function. One should, for example, be able to see that things
are hopeless and yet be determined to make them otherwise.
—F. SCOTT FITZGERALD

•

It is the mark of an educated mind to be able to
entertain a thought without accepting it.
—ARISTOTLE

Humor is a serious thing. I like to think of it as one of our greatest earliest natural resources, which must be preserved at all cost.

—**JAMES THURBER**

•

When you read a classic you do not see in the book more than you did before. You see more in you than there was before.

—**CLIFTON FADIMAN**

•

Mediocrity knows nothing higher than itself, but talent instantly recognizes genius.

—**SIR ARTHUR CONAN DOYLE**

•

Life beats down and crushes the soul, but art reminds you that you have one.

—**STELLA ADLER**

I do not feel obliged to believe that that same God who has endowed us with sense, reason, and intellect has intended us to forgo their use.

—GALILEO GALILEI

Exuberance is beauty.

—WILLIAM BLAKE

Writing is a struggle against silence.

—CARLOS FUENTES

Talk sense to a fool and he calls you foolish.

—EURIPIDES

Education is not the filling of a pail, but the lighting of a fire.
— **WILLIAM BUTLER YEATS**

•

I have always thought the actions of men the
best interpreters of their thoughts.
— **JOHN LOCKE**

•

Perhaps the most valuable result of all education is the
ability to make yourself do the thing you have to do, when
it ought to be done, whether you like it or not.
— **WALTER BAGEHOT**

You cannot teach a man anything; you can
only help him find it within himself.
—GALILEO GALILEI

•

People demand freedom of speech to make up for
the freedom of thought which they avoid.
—SØREN KIERKEGAARD

•

Anyone who conducts an argument by appealing to authority
is not using his intelligence; he is just using his memory.
—LEONARDO DA VINCI

•

Where so many hours have been spent in convincing myself that
I am right, is there not some reason to fear I may be wrong?
—JANE AUSTEN

Prejudices, it is well known, are most difficult to eradicate from the heart whose soil has never been loosened or fertilized by education; they grow there, firm as weeds among rocks.
—CHARLOTTE BRONTË

The test and the use of man's education is that he finds pleasure in the exercise of his mind.
—JACQUES MARTIN BARZUN

I find that a great part of the information I have was acquired by looking up something and finding something else on the way.
—FRANKLIN P. ADAMS

The writer wants to be understood much more than he
wants to be respected or praised or even loved. And that
perhaps, is what makes him different from others.

—LEO C. ROSTEN

Fantasy, abandoned by reason, produces impossible monsters; united
with it, she is the mother of the arts and the origin of marvels.

—FRANCISCO DE GOYA

Paradoxically though it may seem, it is none the less true
that life imitates art far more than art imitates life.

—OSCAR WILDE

Genius is nothing but a great aptitude for patience.

—GEORGES-LOUIS DE BUFFON

People are always so boring when they band together. You have to be alone to develop all the idiosyncrasies that make a person interesting.

—ANDY WARHOL

Creative minds have been known to survive any sort of bad training.

—ANNA FREUD

An intellectual is a man who says a simple thing in a difficult way;
an artist is a man who says a difficult thing in a simple way.

—CHARLES BUKOWSKI

Conception, my boy, fundamental brain work, is what makes all the difference in art. The job of the artist is always to deepen the mystery.

—FRANCIS BACON

Art is made to disturb. Science reassures. There is only one valuable thing in art: the thing you cannot explain.
—GEORGES BRAQUE

•

Precision is not reality.
—HENRI MATISSE

•

Life is brief, art is long.
—HIPPOCRATES

•

The purpose of art is to lay bare the questions which have been hidden by the answers.
—JAMES BALDWIN

The invariable mark of wisdom is to see the miraculous in the common.
—RALPH WALDO EMERSON

Poor is the pupil who does not surpass his master.
—LEONARDO DA VINCI

Lord, grant that I may always desire more than I can accomplish.
—MICHELANGELO

Creativity is allowing yourself to make mistakes.

Art is knowing which ones to keep.
—SCOTT ADAMS

In every man's heart there is a secret nerve that
answers to the vibrations of beauty.
—CHRISTOPHER DARLINGTON MORLEY

Beauty in things lies in the mind which contemplates them.
—DAVID HUME

The best and most beautiful things in life cannot be
seen, not touched, but are felt in the heart.
—HELEN KELLER

There are flowers everywhere, for those who bother to look.
—HENRI MATISSE

God, give us the grace to accept with serenity the things that cannot be changed, the courage to change the things which should be changed, and the wisdom to distinguish the one from the other.
—REINHOLD NIEBUHR

Do not say a little in many words but a great deal in a few.
—PYTHAGORAS

What sculpture is to a block of marble, education is to the soul.
—JOSEPH ADDISON

Real education should educate us out of self into something far

finer; into a selflessness which links us with all humanity.

—LADY NANCY ASTOR

•

To educate a man is to unfit him to be a slave.

—FREDERICK DOUGLASS

•

No man can be called friendless when he has God

and the companionship of good books.

—ELIZABETH BARRETT BROWNING

•

By words the mind is winged.

—ARISTOPHANES

Wise men talk because they have something to say;

fools talk because they have to say something.

—SAUL BELLOW

•

A little learning is a dangerous thing /

Drink deep, or taste not the Pierian spring.

—ALEXANDER POPE

•

Be not a slave of words.

—THOMAS CARLYLE

•

The confidence of ignorance will always

overcome the indecision of knowledge.

—ANONYMOUS

Integrity without knowledge is weak and useless, and knowledge without integrity is dangerous and dreadful.
—SAMUEL JOHNSON

All wish to possess knowledge, but few, comparatively speaking, are willing to pay the price.
—JUVENAL

True wisdom is less presuming than folly. The wise man doubteth often, and changeth his mind; the fool is obstinate, and doubteth not; he knoweth all things but his own ignorance.
—AKHENATEN

What really knocks me out is a book that, when you're all done reading it, you wish the author that wrote it was a terrific friend of yours and you could call him up on the phone whenever you felt like it. That doesn't happen much, though.

—J. D. SALINGER

The art of a people is a true mirror to their minds.

—JAWAHARLAL NEHRU

Genius may have its limitations, but stupidity is not thus handicapped.

—L. RON HUBBARD

He that studieth revenge keepeth his own wounds
green, which otherwise would heal and do well.
—JOHN MILTON

•

The first man to use abusive language instead of
his fists was the founder of civilization.
—SIGMUND FREUD

•

Beware the man of a single book.
—BERTRAND RUSSELL

•

It requires wisdom to understand wisdom;
the music is nothing if the audience is deaf.
—WALTER LIPPMAN

Happy the man who has broken the chains which hurt the
mind, and has given up worrying, once and for all.
—OVID

•

Human history becomes more and more a race
between education and catastrophe.
—H. G. WELLS

•

Genius ain't anything more than elegant common sense.
—JOSH BILLINGS

•

To act with common sense, according to the moment, is
the best wisdom I know and the best philosophy is to do
one's duties, take the world as it comes, submit respectfully
to one's lot; bless the goodness that has given us so much
happiness with it, whatever it is; and despise affectation.
—HORACE WALPOLE

If you make people think they're thinking, they'll love you;
but if you really make them think, they'll hate you.
—DONALD ROBERT PERRY MARQUIS

•

He who asks is a fool for five minutes, but he
who does not ask remains a fool forever.
—CHINESE PROVERB

•

A good listener is not only popular everywhere,
but after a while he gets to know something.
—WILSON MIZNER

•

Education makes a people easy to lead, but difficult to drive;
easy to govern but impossible to enslave.
—LORD HENRY BROUGHAM

A correct answer is like an affectionate kiss.
— **JOHANN WOLFGANG VON GOETHE**

Wisdom is not a product of schooling but of

the lifelong attempt to acquire it.
— **ALBERT EINSTEIN**

A teacher affects eternity; he can never tell, where his influence stops.
— **HENRY BROOKS ADAMS**

To teach is to learn twice.
— **JOSEPH JOUBERT**

Do not quench your inspiration and your imagination;

do not become the slave of your model.

—VINCENT VAN GOGH

•

Style can make complicated things seem

simple, or simple things complicated.

—JEAN COCTEAU

•

Fashions change, but style is forever.

—ANONYMOUS

•

We should be careful to get out of an experience only the wisdom

that is in it—and stop there; lest we be like the cat that sits down on

a hot stove-lid. She will never sit down on a hot stove-lid again—and

that is well; but also she will never sit down on a cold one anymore.

—MARK TWAIN

Truth in science can be defined as the working hypothesis
best suited to open the way to the next better one.
—**KONRAD LORENZ**

The conventional view serves to protect us
from the painful job of thinking.
—**JOHN KENNETH GALBRAITH**

A man thinks that by mouthing hard words
he understands hard things.
—**HERMAN MELVILLE**

The mind is its own place, and in itself,
can make heaven of Hell, and a hell of Heaven.
—**JOHN MILTON**

I quote others only in order the better to express myself.
—**MICHEL DE MONTAIGNE**

•

It is better to be high-spirited even though one makes more
mistakes, than to be narrow-minded and too prudent.
—**VINCENT VAN GOGH**

•

Poetry begins in delight and ends in wisdom.
—**ROBERT FROST**

•

There is no squabbling so violent as that between people who accepted
an idea yesterday and those who will accept the same idea tomorrow.
—**CHRISTOPHER DARLINGTON MORLEY**

A great memory is never made synonymous with wisdom,

any more than a dictionary would be called a treatise.

—JOHN HENRY NEWMAN

●

Wisdom is ofttimes nearer when we stoop / Than when we soar.

—WILLIAM WORDSWORTH

●

True wit is nature to advantage dressed, /

What oft was thought, but ne'er so well expressed.

—ALEXANDER POPE

It is a good thing for an uneducated man to read books of quotations. *Bartlett's Familiar Quotations* is an admirable work, and I studied it intently. The quotations when engraved upon the memory give you good thoughts. They also make you anxious to read the authors and look for more.

—SIR WINSTON CHURCHILL

Almost every wise saying has an opposite one, no less wise, to balance it.

—GEORGE SANTAYANA

Absurdity, n.: A statement or belief manifestly inconsistent with one's own opinion.

—AMBROSE BIERCE

The fool wonders, the wise man asks.

—**BENJAMIN DISRAELI**

•

Complaint always comes back in an echo from the ends of the world; but silence strengthens us.

—**G. K. CHESTERTON**

•

There lives more faith in honest doubt, believe me, than in half the creeds.

—**ALFRED, LORD TENNYSON**

•

The ultimate result of shielding men from the effects of folly, is to fill the world with fools.

—**HERBERT SPENCER**

The liar's punishment is not in the least that he is not
believed, but that he cannot believe anyone else.
— GEORGE BERNARD SHAW

Contradiction is not a sign of falsity, nor the
lack of contradiction a sign of truth.
— BLAISE PASCAL

To be positive: To be mistaken at the top of one's voice.
— AMBROSE BIERCE

I do not agree with what you say, but I will
defend to the death your right to say it.
— VOLTAIRE

I never know whether to pity or congratulate
a man on coming to his senses.
—**WILLIAM MAKEPEACE THACKERAY**

Some books are undeservedly forgotten;
none are undeservedly remembered.
—**W. H. AUDEN**

True words are not always pretty; pretty words are not always true.
—**ANONYMOUS**

Truth lies within a little and certain compass, but error is immense.
—**HENRY ST. JOHN**

Never chase a lie. Let it alone, and it will run itself to death.
—LYMAN BEECHER

A man may learn wisdom even from a foe.
—ARISTOPHANES

Nobody can be so amusingly arrogant as a young man who
has just discovered an old idea and thinks it is his own.
—SYDNEY HARRIS

The opposite of a correct statement is a false statement.
The opposite of a profound truth may well be another profound truth.
—NIELS BOHR

A belief is not true because it is useful.
—HENRI-FRÉDÉRIC AMIEL

●

As scarce as truth is, the supply has always

been in excess of the demand.
—JOSH BILLINGS

●

I do not believe today everything I believed yesterday;
I wonder will I believe tomorrow everything I believe today.
—MATTHEW ARNOLD

●

A belief is not merely an idea the mind possesses;

it is an idea that possesses the mind.
—ROBERT OXTON BOLT

God is in the details.

—**LUDWIG MIES VAN DER ROHE**

•

When a man you like switches from what he said a year ago, or four years ago, he is a broad-minded person who has courage enough to change his mind with changing conditions. When a man you don't like does it, he is a liar who has broken his promises.

—**FRANKLIN P. ADAMS**

•

A lie gets halfway around the world before the truth has a chance to get its pants on.

—**SIR WINSTON CHURCHILL**

Human reason is like a drunken man on horseback;
set it up on one side and it tumbles over on the other.
—MARTIN LUTHER

•

I passionately hate the idea of being with it, I think an
artist has always to be out of step with his time.
—ORSON WELLES

•

Any great work of art revives and readapts time and space,
and the measure of its success is the extent to which it makes
you an inhabitant of that world—the extent to which it
invites you in and lets you breathe its strange, special air.
—LEONARD BERNSTEIN

Those who dream by night in the dusty recesses of their
minds wake in the day to find that all was vanity, but the
dreamers of the day are dangerous men for they may act
their dream with open eyes and make it possible.
—T. E. LAWRENCE

•

Truth that's told with bad intent / Beats all the Lies you can invent.
—WILLIAM BLAKE

•

Keep me away from the wisdom which does not
cry, the philosophy which does not laugh, and the
greatness which does not bow before children.
—KAHLIL GIBRAN

Man's mind, once stretched by a new idea,

never regains its original dimensions.

—OLIVER WENDELL HOLMES JR.

Don't talk unless you can improve the silence.

—JORGE LUIS BORGES

The wastebasket is the writer's best friend.

—ISAAC BASHEVIS SINGER

Where is the wisdom we have lost in knowledge?

Where is the knowledge we have lost in information?

—T. S. ELIOT

Those who will not reason are bigots, those who cannot
are fools, and those who dare not are slaves.
—GEORGE GORDON, LORD BYRON

•

The power of accurate observation is commonly
called cynicism by those who have not got it.
—GEORGE BERNARD SHAW

•

To the artist there is never anything ugly in nature.
—AUGUSTE RODIN

•

Even in the desolate wilderness, stars can still shine.
—AOI JIYUU SHIROI NOZOMI

Peace is not a relationship of nations. It is a condition of mind brought about by a serenity of soul. Peace is not merely the absence of war. It is also a state of mind. Lasting peace can come only to peaceful people.

— JAWAHARLAL NEHRU

The sage wears rough clothing and holds the jewel in his heart.

— LAO-TZU

Heard melodies are sweet, but those unheard / Are sweeter . . .

— JOHN KEATS

Do not the most moving moments of our lives find us all without words?

— MARCEL MARCEAU

It is only by introducing the young to great literature, drama and music, and to the excitement of great science that we open to them the possibilities that lie within the human spirit—enable them to see visions and dream dreams.

—ERIC ANDERSON

●

To conquer fear is the beginning of wisdom.

—BERTRAND RUSSELL

●

Literature adds to reality, it does not simply describe it. It enriches the necessary competencies that daily life requires and provides; and in this respect, it irrigates the deserts that our lives have already become.

—C. S. LEWIS

True wisdom comes to each of us when we realize how little we understand about life, ourselves, and the world around us.

—SOCRATES

•

Writing is an adventure. To begin with, it is a toy and an amusement. Then it becomes a mistress, then it becomes a master, then it becomes a tyrant. The last phase is that just as you are about to be reconciled to your servitude, you kill the monster and fling him to the public.

—SIR WINSTON CHURCHILL

•

Knowledge comes, but wisdom lingers. It may not be difficult to store up in the mind a vast quantity of facts within a comparatively short time, but the ability to form judgments requires the severe discipline of hard work and the tempering heat of experience and maturity.

—CALVIN COOLIDGE

"Google" is not a synonym for "research."
—**DAN BROWN**

Anyone who stops learning is old, whether at twenty
or eighty. Anyone who keeps learning stays young. The
greatest thing in life is to keep your mind young.
—**HENRY FORD**

Wisdom ceases to be wisdom when it becomes too proud to weep,
too grave to laugh, and too selfish to seek other than itself.
—**KAHLIL GIBRAN**

Reading maketh a full man, conference a ready
man, and writing an exact man.
—**SIR FRANCIS BACON**

The mind is everything. What you think you become.

— **BUDDHA**

If thou hast wit & learning, add to it Wisdom and Modesty.

— **BENJAMIN FRANKLIN**

It is the writer's privilege to help man endure by lifting his heart.

— **WILLIAM FAULKNER**

Beware of false knowledge; it is more dangerous than ignorance.

— **GEORGE BERNARD SHAW**

Of all the inanimate objects, of all men's creations, books
are the nearest to us, for they contain our very thoughts,
our ambitions, our indignations, our illusions, our fidelity
to truth, and our persistent leaning toward error.
—JOSEPH CONRAD

•

In a library we are surrounded by many hundreds of dear friends
imprisoned by an enchanter in paper and leathern boxes.
—RALPH WALDO EMERSON

•

Whatever the mind of man can conceive and believe, it can achieve.
—NAPOLEON HILL

•

No one is able to enjoy such feast than the one
who throws a party in his own mind.
—SELMA LAGERLÖF

A nation's treasure is its scholars.

—YIDDISH PROVERB

•

A prudent question is one-half of wisdom.

—SIR FRANCIS BACON

•

The man of action has the present, but the thinker controls the future.

—OLIVER WENDELL HOLMES JR.

•

By three methods we may learn wisdom: First, by reflection,
which is noblest; second, by imitation, which is easiest;
and third by experience, which is the bitterest.

—CONFUCIUS

If you ask me what I came to do in this world,

I, an artist, will answer you: I am here to live out loud.

—ÉMILE ZOLA

•

There is more pleasure to building castles

in the air than on the ground.

—EDWARD GIBBON

•

No man was ever wise by chance.

—SENECA THE ELDER

•

Just as treasures are uncovered from the earth, so virtue appears

from good deeds, and wisdom appears from a pure and peaceful

mind. To walk safely through the maze of human life, one

needs the light of wisdom and the guidance of virtue.

—BUDDHA

V.

∎ ∎ ∎ ∎ ∎ ∎ ∎ ∎ ∎

Politics and Politicians, Government and Statesmen

We the People of the United States, in order to form a more perfect union, establish justice, insure domestic tranquility, provide for the common defense, promote the general welfare, and secure the blessings of liberty to ourselves and our posterity, do ordain and establish this Constitution for the United States of America.

—PREAMBLE TO THE CONSTITUTION OF THE UNITED STATES OF AMERICA

We hold these Truths to be self-evident, that all Men are created equal, that they are endowed by their Creator with certain unalienable Rights, that among these are Life, Liberty and the Pursuit of Happiness . . .

—DECLARATION OF INDEPENDENCE

I have sworn upon the altar of God, eternal hostility against every form of tyranny over the mind of man.

—THOMAS JEFFERSON

All the great things are simple, and many can be expressed in
a single word: freedom; justice; honor; duty; mercy; hope.
—**SIR WINSTON CHURCHILL**

A nation which makes the final sacrifice for
life and freedom does not get beaten.
—**MUSTAFA KEMAL ATATÜRK**

Only our individual faith in freedom can keep us free.
—**DWIGHT D. EISENHOWER**

Is life so dear, or peace so sweet, as to be purchased at the price of
chains and slavery? Forbid it, Almighty God! I know not what course
others may take; but as for me, give me liberty or give me death!
—**PATRICK HENRY**

Those who expect to reap the blessings of freedom must,
like men, undergo the fatigue of supporting it.
—THOMAS PAINE

•

Power tends to corrupt, and absolute power corrupts absolutely.
—LORD ACTON

•

Good order is the foundation of all things.
—EDMUND BURKE

•

Give me the liberty to know, to utter, and to argue freely
according to my conscience, above all liberties.
—JOHN MILTON

All politics is local.

—**THOMAS P. "TIP" O'NEILL JR.**

They that can give up essential liberty to obtain a little temporary safety deserve neither liberty nor safety.

—**BENJAMIN FRANKLIN**

If you once forfeit the confidence of your fellow citizens, you can never regain their respect and esteem. You may fool all of the people some of the time; you can even fool some of the people all the time; but you can't fool all of the people all of the time.

—**ABRAHAM LINCOLN**

The language of the law must not be foreign to
the ears of those who are to obey it.
—LEARNED HAND

•

The conquer'd, also, and enslaved by war,
Shall, with their freedom lost, all virtue lose.
—JOHN MILTON

•

Politics is the art of looking for trouble, finding it whether it exists
or not, diagnosing it incorrectly, and applying the wrong remedy.
—ERNEST BENN

•

The hardest thing about any political campaign is how to
win without proving that you are unworthy of winning.
—THEODOR ADORNO

A society of sheep must in time beget a government of wolves.
—BERTRAND DE JOUVENEL

Freedom is like drink. If you take any at all, you might as
well take enough to make you happy for a while.
—FINLEY PETER DUNNE

If liberty means anything at all, it means the right
to tell people what they do not want to hear.
—GEORGE ORWELL

If we do not believe in freedom of speech for those
we despise we do not believe in it at all.
—NOAM CHOMSKY

Most people do not really want freedom, because freedom involves
responsibility, and most people are frightened of responsibility.
—SIGMUND FREUD

You can only protect your liberties in this world by protecting
the other man's freedom. You can only be free if I am free.
—CLARENCE DARROW

The measure of a man is what he does with power.
—PITTACUS

All that is necessary for the triumph of evil
is that good men do nothing.
—EDMUND BURKE

A single death is a tragedy; a million deaths is a statistic.
—**JOSEPH STALIN**

Mankind is at its best when it is most free. This will be
clear if we grasp the principle of liberty. We must recall that
the basic principle of liberty is freedom of choice, which
saying many have on their lips but few in their minds.
—**DANTE ALIGHIERI**

The buck stops here.
—**HARRY S. TRUMAN**

The first method for estimating the intelligence of a
ruler is to look at the men he has around him.
—NICCOLÒ MACHIAVELLI

•

Being powerful is like being a lady. If you have
to tell people you are—you aren't.
—MARGARET THATCHER

•

A leader or a man of action in a crisis almost always acts
subconsciously and then thinks of the reasons for his action.
—JAWAHARLAL NEHRU

•

Who controls the past controls the future.
Who controls the present controls the past.
—GEORGE ORWELL

It is better to die on your feet than to live on your knees.
—**EMILIANO ZAPATA**

You can discover what your enemy fears most by
observing the means he uses to frighten you.
—**ERIC HOFFER**

The very essence of a free government consists in considering
offices as public trusts, bestowed for the good of the country,
and not for the benefit of an individual or a party.
—**JOHN C. CALHOUN**

The free, exploring mind of the individual human is the
most valuable thing in the world. And this I would fight
for: the freedom of the mind to take any direction it wishes,
undirected. And this I must fight against: any idea, religion,
or government which limits or destroys the individual.

—JOHN STEINBECK

Justice delayed is justice denied.

—LEGAL MAXIM

I only ask to be free. The butterflies are free.

—CHARLES DICKENS

The true greatness of nations is in those qualities which
constitute the greatness of the individual.
—CHARLES SUMNER

The best use of laws is to teach men to
trample bad laws under their feet.
—WENDELL PHILLIPS

Politics is an inexact science.
—OTTO VON BISMARCK

We hold these truths to be self-evident,
that all men and women are created equal.
—ELIZABETH CADY STANTON

No taxation without representation.
—RALLYING CRY OF THE AMERICAN REVOLUTION

•

No man is above the law and no man is below it; nor do we
ask any man's permission when we require him to obey it.
Obedience of the law is demanded; not asked as a favor.
—THEODORE ROOSEVELT

•

I must study politics and war that my sons may have
liberty to study mathematics and philosophy.
—JOHN ADAMS

•

A people that values its privileges above its principles soon loses both.
—DWIGHT D. EISENHOWER

The right to be heard does not automatically
include the right to be taken seriously.
—**HUBERT H. HUMPHREY**

•

The death of democracy is not likely to be an
assassination from ambush. It will be a slow extinction
from apathy, indifference, and undernourishment.
—**ROBERT HUTCHINS**

•

The man who strikes first admits that his ideas have given out.
—**CHINESE PROVERB**

•

It is inaccurate to say I hate everything. I am strongly in favor
of common sense, common honesty, and common decency.
This makes me forever ineligible for any public office.
—**H. L. MENCKEN**

Freedom of thought and the right to private judgment, in matters of conscience, driven from every corner of the earth, direct their course to this happy country as their last asylum. Let us cherish the noble guests, and shelter them under the wings of universal toleration.

—SAMUEL ADAMS

There are few things wholly evil or wholly good. Almost everything, especially of government policy, is an inseparable compound of the two, so that our best judgment of the preponderance between them is continually demanded.

—ABRAHAM LINCOLN

Those who corrupt the public mind are just as evil as those who steal from the public purse.

—ADLAI E. STEVENSON

A man's feet should be planted in his country,

but his eyes should survey the world.

—GEORGE SANTAYANA

In politics stupidity is not a handicap.

—NAPOLÉON BONAPARTE

Nothing in life is certain except death and taxes.

—BENJAMIN FRANKLIN

I expose slavery in this country, because to expose it is to kill it. Slavery

is one of those monsters of darkness to whom the light of truth is death.

—FREDERICK DOUGLASS

The true republic: men, their rights and nothing more; women, their rights and nothing less.
—FRANKLIN P. ADAMS

I know not with what weapons World War III will be fought, but World War IV will be fought with sticks and stones.
—ALBERT EINSTEIN

Practical politics consists in ignoring facts.
—HENRY BROOKS ADAMS

Even when laws have been written down, they ought not always to remain unaltered.
—ARISTOTLE

Toleration is good for all, or it is good for none.
— E D M U N D   B U R K E

•

The whole history of the progress of human liberty shows
that all concessions yet made to her august claims have been
born of earnest struggle. . . . If there is no struggle, there is no
progress. Those who profess to favor freedom, and yet deprecate
agitation, are men who want crops without plowing up the
ground, they want rain without thunder and lightning. They
want the ocean without the awful roar of its many waters.
— F R E D E R I C K   D O U G L A S S

•

In the country of the blind the one-eyed man is king.
— D E S I D E R I U S   E R A S M U S

The Law, in its majestic equality, forbids the rich, as well as the poor, to sleep under the bridges, to beg in the streets, and to steal bread.
— ANATOLE FRANCE

•

Cautious, careful people always casting about to preserve their reputation or social standards never can bring about reform. Those who are really in earnest are willing to be anything or nothing in the world's estimation, and publicly and privately, in season and out, avow their sympathies with despised ideas and their advocates, and bear the consequences.
— SUSAN B. ANTHONY

•

One man with courage is a majority.
— THOMAS JEFFERSON

•

Injustice anywhere is a threat to justice everywhere.
— MARTIN LUTHER KING JR.

Let the word go forth from this time and place, to friend and foe alike, that the torch has been passed to a new generation of Americans—born in this century, tempered by war, disciplined by a hard and bitter peace, proud of our ancient heritage—and unwilling to witness or permit the slow undoing of those human rights to which this Nation has always been committed, and to which we are committed today at home and around the world.

Let every nation know, whether it wishes us well or ill, that we shall pay any price, bear any burden, meet any hardship, support any friend, oppose any foe, in order to assure the survival and the success of liberty.

So let us begin anew—remembering on both sides that civility is not a sign of weakness, and sincerity is always subject to proof. Let us never negotiate out of fear. But let us never fear to negotiate.

All this will not be finished in the first 100 days. Nor will it be finished in the first 1,000 days, nor in the life of this Administration, nor even perhaps in our lifetime on this planet. But let us begin.

And so, my fellow Americans: ask not what your country can do for you—ask what you can do for your country.

—JOHN F. KENNEDY

If mankind minus one were of one opinion, then mankind
is no more justified in silencing the one than the one—if he
had the power—would be justified in silencing mankind.
— JOHN STUART MILL

•

The politician is . . . trained in the art of inexactitude.
His words tend to be blunt or rounded, because if they have
a cutting edge they may later return to wound him.
— EDWARD R. MURROW

•

Bad officials are elected by good citizens who do not vote.
— GEORGE JEAN NATHAN

•

War is delightful to those who have had no experience of it.
— DESIDERIUS ERASMUS

You cannot simultaneously prevent and prepare for war.
—ALBERT EINSTEIN

Man's capacity for justice makes democracy possible;
but man's inclination to injustice makes democracy necessary.
—REINHOLD NIEBUHR

The nine most terrifying words in the English language
are, "I'm from the government and I'm here to help."
—RONALD REAGAN

Laws do not persuade just because they threaten.
—SENECA THE ELDER

If you can't stand the heat, get out of the kitchen.
—**HARRY S. TRUMAN**

•

Politicians are the same all over. They promise to
build bridges even when there are no rivers.
—**NIKITA KHRUSHCHEV**

•

One cool judgment is worth a dozen hasty councils.
The thing to do is to supply light and not heat.
—**WOODROW WILSON**

•

Rebellion to tyrants is obedience to God.
—**THOMAS JEFFERSON**

•

If the misery of the poor be caused not by the laws of
nature, but by our institutions, great is our sin.
—**CHARLES DARWIN**

Law is order, and good law is good order.

— ARISTOTLE

•

Man is born free; and everywhere he is in chains. One thinks himself the master of others, and still remains a greater slave than they. How did this change come about? I do not know. What can make it legitimate? That question I think I can answer. If I took into account only force, and the effects derived from it, I should say: As long as a people is compelled to obey, and obeys, it does well; as soon as it can shake off the yoke, and shakes it off, it does still better; for, regaining its liberty by the same right as took it away, either it is justified in resuming it, or there was no justification for those who took it away. But the social order is a sacred right which is the basis of all other rights. Nevertheless, this right does not come from nature, and must therefore be founded on conventions.

— JEAN-JACQUES ROUSSEAU

Liberty is the right to silence.
—GRAFFITI DURING FRENCH STUDENT RIOTS, 1968

•

In some cases non-violence requires more militancy than violence.
—CÉSAR CHÁVEZ

•

In the province of the mind, what one believes
to be true either is true or becomes true.
—JOHN LILLY

•

Freedom . . . is not ours by inheritance; it must be fought
for and defended constantly by each generation, for it
comes only once to a people. Those who have known
freedom, and then lost it, have never known it again.
—RONALD REAGAN

In the future days, which we seek to make secure, we look forward to a world founded upon four essential human freedoms. The first is freedom of speech and expression—everywhere in the world. The second is freedom of every person to worship God in his own way—everywhere in the world. The third is freedom from want—which, translated into world terms, means economic understandings which will secure to every nation a healthy peacetime life for its inhabitants—everywhere in the world. The fourth is freedom from fear—which, translated into world terms, means a world-wide reduction of armaments to such a point and in such a thorough fashion that no nation will be in a position to commit an act of physical aggression against any neighbor—anywhere in the world.

—FRANKLIN DELANO ROOSEVELT

•

Of all times in time of war the press should be free.

—WILLIAM BORAH

The greatest dangers to liberty lurk in insidious encroachment by men of zeal, well-meaning, but without understanding.
—**LOUIS D. BRANDEIS**

You have not converted a man because you have silenced him.
—**VISCOUNT JOHN MORLEY**

I know war as few men now living know it, and nothing to me is more revolting. I have long advocated its complete abolition, as its very destructiveness on both friend and foe has rendered it useless as a means of settling international disputes.
—**DOUGLAS MACARTHUR**

If a nation values anything more than freedom, it will
lose its freedom; and the irony of it is that if it is comfort
or money that it values more, it will lose that too.
—W. SOMERSET MAUGHAM

•

Freedom is not worth having if it does not connote freedom
to err. It passes my comprehension how human beings,
be they ever so experienced and able, can delight in
depriving other human beings of that precious right.
—MOHANDAS GANDHI

•

The punishment which the wise suffer who refuse to take part in
the government, is to live under the government of worse men.
—PLATO

To give up the task of reforming society is to give
up one's responsibility as a free man.
—ALAN PATON

•

We learn from history that we do not learn from history.
—GEORG WILHELM FRIEDRICH HEGEL

•

Man does not live by words alone, despite the
fact that sometimes he has to eat them.
—ADLAI E. STEVENSON

•

The most effective way of attacking vice is to expose it
to public ridicule. People can put up with rebukes, but
they cannot bear being laughed at: they are prepared to
be wicked but they dislike appearing ridiculous.
—MOLIÈRE

Freedom is man's capacity to take a hand in his own development. It is our capacity to mold ourselves.

—ROLLO MAY

When people are free to do as they please, they usually imitate each other.

—ERIC HOFFER

The united voice of millions cannot lend the smallest foundation to falsehood.

—OLIVER GOLDSMITH

When you are right, you cannot be too radical; when you are wrong, you cannot be too conservative.

—MARTIN LUTHER KING JR.

Heresy is another word for freedom of thought.
—GRAHAM GREENE

A government that is big enough to give you all
you want is big enough to take it all away.
—BARRY GOLDWATER

Men are not hanged for stealing horses,
but that horses may not be stolen.
—GEORGE SAVILE

The basis of our political system is the right of the people to
make and to alter their constitutions of government.
—GEORGE WASHINGTON

Freedom of the mind requires not only, or not even
specially, the absence of legal constraints but the presence
of alternative thoughts. The most successful tyranny is not
the one that uses force to assure uniformity but the one
that removes the awareness of other possibilities.

—ALAN BLOOM

The hottest places in hell are reserved for those who in
times of great moral crises maintain their neutrality.

—DANTE ALIGHIERI

America will never be destroyed from the outside. If we falter and
lose our freedoms, it will be because we destroyed ourselves.

—ABRAHAM LINCOLN

No one flower can ever symbolize this nation. America is a bouquet.

—WILLIAM SAFIRE

Genuine politics—every politics worthy of the name—
the only politics I am willing to devote myself to—is
simply a matter of serving those around us: serving the
community and serving those who will come after us.
— **VÁCLAV HAVEL**

The true test of the American ideal is whether we're able
to recognize our failings and then rise together to meet the
challenges of our time. Whether we allow ourselves to be shaped
by events and history, or whether we act to shape them.
— **BARACK OBAMA**

A politician thinks of the next election.
A statesman, of the next generation.
— **JAMES FREEMAN CLARKE**

You can't hold a man down without staying down with him.
— **BOOKER T. WASHINGTON**

When we lose the right to be different, we lose the privilege to be free.
—**CHARLES EVANS HUGHES**

When will our consciences grow so tender that we will

act to prevent human misery rather than avenge it?
—**ELEANOR ROOSEVELT**

Our species needs, and deserves, a citizenry with minds wide

awake and a basic understanding of how the world works.
—**CARL SAGAN**

This is how change happens, though. It is a relay race, and we're very conscious of that, that our job really is to do our part of the race, and then we pass it on, and then someone picks it up, and it keeps going. And that is how it is. And we can do this, as a planet, with the consciousness that we may not get it, you know, today, but there's always a tomorrow.

—**ALICE WALKER**

•

I can assure you, public service is a stimulating, proud and lively enterprise. It is not just a way of life, it is a way to live fully. Its greatest attraction is the sheer challenge of it— struggling to find solutions to the great issues of the day. It can fulfill your highest aspirations. The call to service is one of the highest callings you will hear and your country can make.

—**LEE HAMILTON, 9/11 COMMISSION CHAIRMAN**

This is man's highest end, to others' service, all his powers to bend.
—SOPHOCLES

There is no greater calling than to serve your fellow men.
There is no greater contribution than to help the weak. There
is no greater satisfaction than to have done it well.
—WALTER REUTHER

Do nothing—Or, take history into our own hands
and like few generations are given the chance, bend
it, bend it, in the service of a better day.
—JOE BIDEN

Justice is never given; it is exacted and the struggle must be
continuous for freedom is never a final fact, but a continuing
evolving process to higher and higher levels of human,
social, economic, political and religious relationship.
—A. PHILIP RANDOLPH

Every difference of opinion is not a difference of principle.
We have called by different names brethren of the same principle.
—**THOMAS JEFFERSON**

Half of the American people have never read a newspaper.
Half never voted for president. One hopes it is the same half.
—**GORE VIDAL**

Where is the man who owes nothing to the land in which he lives?
Whatever that land may be, he owes to it the most precious thing
possessed by man, the morality of his actions and the love of virtue.
—**JEAN-JACQUES ROUSSEAU**

The life of the nation is secure only while the
nation is honest, truthful, and virtuous.
—**FREDERICK DOUGLASS**

•

Volunteers are the only human beings on the face of
the earth who reflect this nation's compassion, unselfish
caring, patience, and just plain love for one another.
—**ERMA BOMBECK**

•

The right way is not always the popular and easy way. Standing
for right when it is unpopular is a true test of moral character.
—**MARGARET CHASE SMITH**

We know that government can't solve all our problems—and we don't want it to. But we also know that there are some things we can't do on our own. We know that there are some things we do better together.

—**BARACK OBAMA**

VI.

- - - - - - - - - -

Proverbial Wisdom

A country can be judged by the quality of its proverbs.
— GERMAN PROVERB

A handful of patience is worth more than a bushel of brains.
— DUTCH PROVERB

It is easy to despise what you cannot get.
— AESOP, "THE FOX AND THE GRAPES"
(the origin of the phrase "sour grapes")

A quiet fool is half a sage.

—YIDDISH PROVERB

A bird in the hand is worth two in the bush.

—ENGLISH PROVERB

It is thrifty to prepare today for the wants of tomorrow.

—AESOP, "THE ANT AND THE GRASSHOPPER"

Union gives strength.

—AESOP, "THE BUNDLE OF STICKS"

If you want to give God a good laugh, tell Him your plans.

—YIDDISH PROVERB

Please all, and you will please none.

—AESOP, "THE MAN, THE BOY, AND THE DONKEY"

Since the house is on fire, let us warm ourselves.

—ITALIAN PROVERB

●

People often grudge others what they cannot enjoy themselves.

—AESOP, "THE DOG IN THE MANGER"

●

We often give our enemies the means of our own destruction.

—AESOP, "THE EAGLE AND THE ARROW"

It is easy to be brave from a safe distance.
—AESOP, "THE WOLF AND THE KID"

Don't think there are no crocodiles because the water is calm.
—MALAYAN PROVERB

Do not count your chickens before they are hatched.
—AESOP, "THE MILK WOMAN AND HER PAIL"

A journey of a thousand miles begins with a single step.

—CHINESE PROVERB

An army of sheep led by a lion would defeat
an army of lions led by a sheep.

—ARAB PROVERB

Procrastination is the thief of time.

—PROVERB FOUND IN MANY CULTURES

Beware lest you lose the substance by grasping at the shadow.
—AESOP, "THE DOG AND THE SHADOW"

•

Luck is like having a rice dumpling fly into your mouth.
—JAPANESE PROVERB

•

The best armor is to keep out of range.
—ITALIAN PROVERB

•

Men often applaud an imitation, and hiss the real thing.
—AESOP, "THE BUFFOON AND THE COUNTRYMAN"

Better to light a candle than to curse the darkness.

—CHINESE PROVERB

When spiders unite, they can tie down a lion.

—ETHIOPIAN PROVERB

Love is friendship set on fire.

—FRENCH PROVERB

The death of a friend is equivalent to the loss of a limb.
—GERMAN PROVERB

•

Dance as if no one's watching, sing as if no one's
listening, and live every day as if it were your last.
—IRISH PROVERB

•

The reverse side also has a reverse side.
—JAPANESE PROVERB

At the end of the game, the king and the

pawn go back in the same box.

—ITALIAN PROVERB

The older the fiddle, the sweeter the tune.

—IRISH PROVERB

Vision without action is daydream. Action without vision is nightmare.

—JAPANESE PROVERB

The generous and bold have the best lives.

—NORWEGIAN PROVERB

Fear is only as deep as the mind allows.
— JAPANESE PROVERB

Turn your face to the sun and the shadows fall behind you.
— MAORI PROVERB

To be damned by the devil is to be truly blessed.
— CHINESE PROVERB

It is better to live one day as a lion, than a thousand days as a lamb.

—ROMAN PROVERB

The church is close, but the road is icey.

The tavern is far, but I will walk carefully.

—RUSSIAN PROVERB

Water that does not move, is always shallow.

—SAMI PROVERB

He who allows his day to pass by without practicing

generosity and enjoying life's pleasures is like a

blacksmith's bellows—he breathes but does not live.

—SANSKRIT PROVERB

Be humble for you are made of earth. Be

noble for you are made of stars.

—SERBIAN PROVERB

It takes an entire village to raise a child.

—AFRICAN PROVERB

Fear less, hope more; eat less, chew more; whine less, breathe more;
talk less, say more; hate less, love more; and all good things are yours.
—SWEDISH PROVERB

Slow and steady wins the race.
—AESOP, "THE TORTOISE AND THE HARE"

By asking for the impossible, obtain the best possible.
—ITALIAN PROVERB

Call on God, but row away from the rocks.

—INDIAN PROVERB

If you must play, decide on three things at the start: the
rules of the game, the stakes, and the quitting time.

—CHINESE PROVERB

Even a clock that does not work is right twice a day.

—POLISH PROVERB

He who hurries cannot walk with dignity.

—CHINESE PROVERB

•

Don't throw away the old bucket until you know
whether the new one holds water.

—SWEDISH PROVERB

•

It's the final straw that broke the camel's back.

—ENGLISH PROVERB

Tell me and I'll forget. Show me, and I may not
remember. Involve me, and I'll understand.
—NATIVE AMERICAN PROVERB

What's good for the goose is good for the gander.
—ENGLISH PROVERB

He who lies down with dogs, rises with fleas.
—ENGLISH PROVERB

A man is not honest simply because he never had a chance to steal.

— RUSSIAN PROVERB

The innkeeper loves the drunkard, but not for a son-in-law.

— YIDDISH PROVERB

Time and words can't be recalled, even if it was only yesterday.

— ESTONIAN PROVERB

You won't help shoots grow by pulling them up higher.
—CHINESE PROVERB

•

Cursing the weather is never good farming.
—ENGLISH PROVERB

•

Too many cooks spoil the broth.
—ENGLISH PROVERB

•

Ask the experienced rather than the learned.
—ARABIC PROVERB

Waste not, want not.

—PROVERB FOUND IN MANY CULTURES

Tomorrow is often the busiest time of the year.

—SPANISH PROVERB

When I rest, I rust.

—GERMAN PROVERB

Revenge is a dish best served cold.
—ITALIAN PROVERB

He who is outside his door has the hardest

part of his journey behind him.
—FLEMISH PROVERB

Nobody's sweetheart is ugly.
—DUTCH PROVERB

The wagon rests in winter, the sleigh in summer, the horse never.
—YIDDISH PROVERB

Birds of a feather flock together.
—ENGLISH PROVERB

Lend a horse, and you may have back his skin.
—ENGLISH PROVERB

You can't hatch chickens from fried eggs.
—GERMAN PROVERB

Care, and not fine stables, makes a good horse.

—DANISH PROVERB

Trees often transplanted seldom prosper.

—FLEMISH PROVERB

Roasted pigeons will not fly into one's mouth.

—DUTCH PROVERB

The early bird catches the worm.

—ENGLISH PROVERB

One meets his destiny often in the road he takes to avoid it.

—FRENCH PROVERB

When the cat's away, the mice will play.

—FRENCH PROVERB

All cats appear grey in the dark.
—ENGLISH PROVERB

•

Curiosity killed the cat.
—ENGLISH PROVERB

•

You can't dance at two weddings at the same time;
nor can you sit on two horses with one behind.
—YIDDISH PROVERB

When rats infest the palace, a lame cat is better than the swiftest horse.

—CHINESE PROVERB

Let sleeping dogs lie.

—FRENCH PROVERB

There are plenty more fish in the sea.

—ENGLISH PROVERB

Whoever gossips to you will gossip about you.

—SPANISH PROVERB

•

Don't change horses in the middle of the stream.

—DUTCH PROVERB

•

You can lead a horse to water, but you can't make him drink.

—ENGLISH PROVERB

It's too late to close the stable door after the horse has bolted.

—FRENCH PROVERB

Even the candle seller dies in the dark.

—COLOMBIAN PROVERB

A road to a friend's house is never long.

—DANISH PROVERB

Speak silver, reply gold.
—SWAHILI PROVERB

When two elephants fight it is the grass that suffers.
—AFRICAN PROVERB

He who does nothing makes no mistakes.
—ITALIAN PROVERB

When one door shuts, a hundred open.

—SPANISH PROVERB

The greedy man stores all but friendship.

—IRISH PROVERB

If a little money does not go out, great money will not come in.

—CHINESE PROVERB

A people without history is like the wind on the buffalo grass.

—LAKOTA SIOUX PROVERB

Joy shared is twice the joy. Sorrow shared is half the sorrow.

—SWEDISH PROVERB

Least said, soonest mended.

—IRISH PROVERB

A rich child often sits in a poor mother's lap.

—DANISH PROVERB

A fool and his money are soon parted.

—ENGLISH PROVERB

Worry gives a small thing a big shadow.

—SWEDISH PROVERB

The gods help them that help themselves.
—AESOP, "HERCULES AND THE WAGGONER"

Sparrows that emulate peacocks are likely to break a thigh.
—BURMESE PROVERB

Do not judge a man until you have walked two moons in his moccasins.
—NATIVE AMERICAN PROVERB

However long the night, the dawn will break.
—AFRICAN PROVERB

Appearances often are deceiving.
—AESOP, "THE WOLF AND THE LAMB"

Big mouthfuls often choke.
—ITALIAN PROVERB

Familiarity breeds contempt.
—AESOP, "THE FOX AND THE LION"

Pride goeth before destruction, and haughty spirit before a fall.
—THE BIBLE, PROVERBS 16:18

●

If you want people to think you are wise, agree with them.
—YIDDISH PROVERB

●

Blessed is the man who can laugh at himself,

for he will never cease to be amused.

—PROVERB FOUND IN MANY CULTURES

God is good, but never dance in a small boat.
—IRISH PROVERB

He that finds discontentment in one place is
not likely to find happiness in another.
—AESOP'S FABLES, "THE ASS AND HIS MASTERS"

To know the road ahead, ask those coming back.
—CHINESE PROVERB

A bad rower blames the oar.

—ICELANDIC PROVERB

•

Men often bear little grievances with less
courage than they do large misfortunes.

—AESOP'S FABLES, "THE ASS AND THE FROGS"

•

Something worth taking is worth asking for.

—GAELIC PROVERB

It is better to have less thunder in the mouth
and more lightning in the hand.
—APACHE PROVERB

When you throw dirt, you lose ground.
—COWBOY SAYING

One day chicken, the next day feathers.
—AMERICAN PROVERB

Dig the well before you are thirsty.
—CHINESE PROVERB

•

Don't look where you fall, but where you slipped.
—AFRICAN PROVERB

•

You've got to do your own growing, no matter
how tall your grandfather was.
—IRISH PROVERB

Fine feathers don't make fine birds.

—AESOP'S FABLES, "THE PEACOCK AND THE CRANE"

•

Words are like eggs: when they are hatched they have wings.

—MALAGASY PROVERB

•

It's better to be a has-been that a never-was.

—COWBOY SAYING

A wise man doesn't need advice, and a fool won't take it.
—ENGLISH PROVERB

God could not be everywhere, so He made mothers.
—JEWISH PROVERB

Even as the archer loves the arrow that flies, so too
he loves the bow that remains constant.
—AFRICAN PROVERB

There is no bad weather, only bad clothing.
—SWEDISH PROVERB

•

It's not enough to know how to ride—you must also know how to fall.
—MEXICAN PROVERB

•

Don't sell your mule to buy a plough.
—AMERICAN PROVERB

Don't skin the bear before it's been shot.
—FINNISH PROVERB

If you find yourself in a hole, the first thing to do is stop diggin'.
—COWBOY SAYING

Think of your faults the first part of the night when you are awake, and
the faults of others the latter part of the night when you are asleep.
—CHINESE PROVERB

Do not fall before you are pushed.

—ENGLISH PROVERB

If you cannot bite, never show your teeth.

—DANISH PROVERB

If you get to thinkin' you're a person of some influence,

try orderin' somebody else's dog around.

—COWBOY SAYING

SELECTED QUOTED SOURCES

Abdul-Jabbar, Kareem (b. 1947), American basketball player

Acheson, Dean (1893–1971), American secretary of state

Acton, Lord (John Dalberg-Acton) (1834–1902), British historian, politician, and author

Adams, Franklin P. (1881–1960), American author and newspaper columnist

Adams, Henry Brooks (1838–1918), American historian

Adams, John (1735–1826), second U.S. president

Adams, Samuel (1722–1803), American statesman

Adams, Scott (b. 1957), American cartoonist and creator of "Dilbert"

Addison, Joseph (1672–1719), English essayist, poet, statesman

Adler, Stella (1901–1992), American stage actress

Adorno, Theodor (1903–1969), German philosopher and sociologist

Aeschylus (525–456 BC), Greek tragic dramatist

Aesop (c. 620 BC–564 BC), Greek fabulist

Akhenaten (d. c. 1354 BC), Egyptian king

Alcott, Bronson (1799–1888), American educational and social reformer

Alcott, Louisa May (1832–1888), American novelist

Algren, Nelson (1909–1981), American novelist

Ali, Muhammad (1942–2016), American boxer

Alighieri, Dante (1265–1321), Italian poet

Allen, Woody (b. 1935), American comedian, actor, and producer

Amiel, Henri-Frédéric (1821–1881), Swiss philosopher and poet

Angelou, Maya, (1928–2014), American author, poet laureate, and composer

Anouilh, Jean (1910–1987), French playwright

Anthony, Susan B. (1820–1906), American women's suffrage leader

Archimedes (287 BC–212 BC), Greek physicist and mathematician

Aristophanes (c. 448 BC–c. 388 BC), Athenian playwright

Aristotle (384 BC–322 BC), Greek philosopher

Arnold, Matthew (1822–1888), British poet and critic

Asimov, Isaac (1920–1992), Russian-American science-fiction writer and scientist

Assisi, Saint Francis of (1182–1226), founder of the Franciscan order

Astaire, Fred (1899–1987), American dancer and actor

Astor, Lady Nancy (1879–1964), English politician

Atatürk, Mustafa Kemal (1881–1938), Turkish soldier and founder of modern Turkey

Athenaeus, second- to third-century Greek grammarian and rhetorician

Auden, W(ystan) H(ugh) (1907–1973), British-American writer and critic

Audubon, John James (1785–1851), French-American naturalist and
  painter
Augustine, Saint (354 AD–430 AD), Early Christian theologian and
  bishop
Aurelius, Marcus (121 AD–180 AD), Roman emperor
Austen, Jane (1775–1817), British writer
Bach, Richard (b. 1936), American writer
Bacon, Francis (1909–1992), Irish artist
Bacon, Sir Francis (1561–1626), philosopher and essayist
Bagehot, Walter (1826–1877), British journalist and economist
Bailey, Pearl (1918–1990), American singer and actress
Baldwin, James (1924–1987), American critic and writer
Ball, Lucille (1911–1989), American actress and comedienne
Balzac, Honoré de (1799–1850), French writer
Bannister, Roger (b. 1929), British long-distance runner
Battista, Orlando (1917–1995), Canadian-American chemist and
  author
Barrie, Sir James Matthew (1860–1937), British writer
Barton, Bruce (1886–1967), American congressman
Baruch, Bernard Mannes (1870–1965), American political advisor
  and stockbroker
Barzun, Jacques Martin (1907–2012), American educator
Beckett, Samuel (1906–1989), Irish dramatist

Beecher, Lyman (1775–1863), American Presbyterian clergyman

Bellow, Saul (1915–2005), American novelist

Benn, Ernest (1875–1954), English publisher

Bennett, Arnold (Enoch) (1867–1931), British novelist

Bennett, William John (b. 1943), U.S. secretary of education

Bennis, Warren G. (1925–2015), American educator and sociologist

Bernhardt, Sarah (1844–1923), French stage and early film star

Bernstein, Leonard (1918–1990), American composer

Berra, Laurence "Yogi" (1925–2015), American baseball player

Besant, Sir Walter (1836–1901), English novelist and humanitarian

Biden, Joe (b. 1942), U.S. vice president and senator

Bierce, Ambrose (1842–1914), American journalist

Billings, Josh (1818–1885), American humorous essayist

Blake, Eubie (1883–1983), American ragtime pianist and composer

Blake, William (1757–1827), British poet

Bloom, Alan (1930–1992), American sociologist and writer

Bohr, Niels (1885–1962), Danish physicist

Boileau, Nicolas (1636–1711), French literary critic and poet

Bolt, Robert Oxton (1924–1995), English author

Bombeck, Erma (Louise) (1927–1996), American author

Bonaparte, Napoléon (1769–1821), French general

Boorstin, Daniel J. (1914–2004), U.S. librarian of Congress

Borah, William (1865–1940), U.S. senator

Borge, Victor (1909–2000), Danish-American pianist and comedian

Borges, Jorge Luis (1899–1986), Argentinian writer

Bowen, Catherine Drinker (1897–1973), American writer

Bradbury, Ray (1920–2012), American science-fiction writer

Brandeis, Louis D. (1856–1941), U.S. Supreme Court justice

Braque, Georges (1882–1963), French painter

Brecht, Bertolt (1898–1956), German playwright

Brinkley, David (1920–2003), American newscaster and commentator

Brontë, Charlotte (1816–1855), British novelist

Brontë, Emily (1818–1848), British novelist

Brothers, Dr. Joyce (1929–2013), American psychologist

Brougham, Lord Henry (1778–1868), British statesman

Brown, Dan (b. 1964), American author

Brown, James (1933–2006), American soul singer

Browning, Elizabeth Barrett (1806–1861), British poet

Browning, Robert (1812–1889), British poet

Bryan, William Jennings (1860–1925), American lawyer and
  politician

Bryant, William Cullen (1794–1878), American poet and newspaper
  editor

Buck, Pearl S. (1892–1973), American missionary and writer

Buddha, Siddhártha Gautama (c. 563 BC–c. 483 BC), founder of
  Buddhism

Bukowski, Charles (1920–1994), German-American poet and novelist

Bulwer-Lytton, Edward George (1803–1873), British novelist and poet

Burke, Edmund (1729–1797), British political writer and statesman

Burnett, Leo (1891–1971), advertising executive

Buscaglia, Leo (1924–1998), American educator

Bush, Barbara (b. 1925), American first lady

Butler, Samuel (1612–1680), English poet and author

Byrnes, James F. (1879–1972), U.S. secretary of state

Byron, George Gordon, Lord (1788–1824), English romantic poet

Campbell, Joseph (1904–1987), American mythologist

Camus, Albert (1913–1960), French existential philosopher and
writer

Capone, Al (1899–1947), Italian-American organized crime boss

Capra, Frank (1897–1991), American film director

Carlyle, Thomas (1795–1881), British historian

Carnegie, Dale (1888–1955), American self-improvement author

Carroll, Lewis (1832–1898), British writer

Carver, George Washington (1864–1943), American agricultural
chemist and inventor

Carver, Raymond (1938–1988), American short story writer and poet

Cervantes, Miguel de (1547–1616), Spanish writer

Chaplin, Charlie (1889–1977), English silent-film actor

Chávez, César (1927–1993), American agrarian labor leader

Chesterfield, Philip Dormer Stanhope, Lord (1694–1773), English
writer and politician

Chesterton, G. K. (1874–1936), English author

Chomsky, Noam (b. 1928), educator, linguist, and political writer

Christie, Agatha (1890–1976), English mystery writer

Churchill, Sir Winston (1874–1965), English prime minister

Ciardi, John (1916–1986), American poet and translator

Cicero, Marcus Tullius (106 BC–43 BC), Roman orator

Clarke, James Freeman (1810–1888), American theologian and author

Clinton, Hillary Rodham (b. 1947), U.S. senator, secretary of state, and presidential candidate

Cocteau, Jean (1889–1963), French avant-garde writer, filmmaker, and artist

Coelho, Paulo (b. 1947), Brazilian lyricist and author

Coleridge, Samuel Taylor (1772–1834), English romantic poet

Colton, Charles Caleb (1780–1832), American clergyman and writer

Conan Doyle, Sir Arthur (1859–1930), British author, creator of Sherlock Holmes

Confucius (c. 551 BC–479 BC), Chinese philosopher

Conrad, Joseph (1857–1924), British novelist

Conroy, Pat (1945–2016), American writer

Cooke, Alistair (1908–2004), British-American journalist and radio/ TV personality

Coolidge, Calvin (1872–1933), thirtieth U.S. president

Cousins, Norman (1915–1990), American editor and author

Crawford, Joan (1905–1977), American film actress

Crisp, Quentin (1908–1999), English autobiographer

Crumb, Robert (b. 1943), social and political cartoonist

cummings, e. e. (1894–1962), American author

da Vinci, Leonardo (1492–1519), Italian artist and innovator

Dalai Lama (b. 1935), Tibetan religious leader

Darrow, Clarence (1857–1938), American lawyer

Darwin, Charles (1809–1882), English naturalist and evolutionary
theorist

Davies, Robertson (1913–1995), Canadian novelist

Davis, Bette (1908–1989), American film actress

Davis, Jefferson (1808–1889), president of the Confederacy during the
Civil War

Davis, Miles Jr. (1926–1991), American jazz musician

de Bergerac, Cyrano (1619–1655), large-nosed French writer

de Buffon, Georges-Louis (1707–1788), French naturalist and author

de Bussy-Rabutin, Comte Roger (1618–1693), French satirical writer

de Jouvenel, Bertrand (1903–1987), French writer

de La Rochefoucauld, François (1613–1680), French author

DeMille, Cecil B. (1881–1959), film director and producer

de Montaigne, Michel (1533–1592), French essayist

Demosthenes (384 BC–322 BC), Greek orator

Deng Xiaoping (1904–1997), Chinese revolutionary and government
leader

Desbordes-Valmore, Marceline (1786–1859), French poet and
   novelist
Descartes, René (1596–1650), French philosopher and mathematician
Dewey, John (1859–1952), American philosopher and educator
Dickens, Charles (1812–1870), English novelist
Dickinson, Emily (1830–1886), American poet
Disraeli, Benjamin (1804–1881), British prime minister and author
Donne, John (1572–1631), British metaphysical poet
Dostoyevsky, Fyodor Mikhailovich (1821–1881), Russian novelist
Douglass, Frederick (1817–1895), American abolitionist, author, and
   orator
Dryden, John (1631–1700), English poet laureate
Dumas, Alexandre (1802–1870), French author
Dunne, Finley Peter (1867–1936), American humorist
Durant, Will (1885–1981), American historian and essayist
Dylan, Bob (b. 1941), American songwriter
Earhart, Amelia (1897–1937), American aviator and author
Edel, Leon (1907–1997), American biographer and critic
Edison, Thomas Alva (1847–1931), American inventor
Einstein, Albert (1879–1955), Austrian-American theoretical
   physicist
Eisenhower, Dwight D. (1890–1969), thirty-fourth U.S. president
Eliot, George, pseudonym of Mary Ann Evans (1819–1880), English
   novelist

Eliot, T. S. (1885–1968), British poet and winner of the Nobel Prize
  for Literature

Ellington, Duke (1899–1974), American jazz musician

Emerson, Ralph Waldo (1803–1882), American philosopher and poet

Epictetus (c. 50 AD–c. 138 AD), Phrygian Stoic philosopher

Epicurus (341 BC–270 BC), Greek philosopher

Erasmus, Desiderius (c. 1466–1536), Dutch Renaissance theologian

Ertz, Susan (1894–1985), British novelist

Euripides (c. 480 BC–406 BC), Greek dramatist

Evert, Chris (b. 1954), American tennis player

Fadiman, Clifton (1904–1999), American literary critic

Faulkner, William (1897–1962), American author and Nobel Prize
  winner

Fenwick, Millicent (1910–1992), American diplomat and
  congresswoman

Feynman, Richard (1918–1988), American physicist

Fitzgerald, F. Scott (1896–1940), American novelist

Fitzgerald, Zelda (1900–1948), American socialite and novelist

Flagg, Fannie (b. 1944), American author

Forbes, Malcolm (1919–1990), American magazine publisher

Ford, Henry (1863–1947), American automobile manufacturer

Forster, E(dward) M(organ) (1879–1970), British author

France, Anatole (1844–1924), French writer and critic

Frank, Anne (1929–1945), Dutch World War II diarist

Franklin, Benjamin (1706–1790), American statesman and writer

Freud, Anna (1895–1982), British psychoanalyst and daughter of Sigmund Freud

Freud, Sigmund (1856–1939), Austrian psychoanalyst

Fromm, Erich (1900–1980), German psychoanalyst and author

Fromme, Dr. Allan (1915–2003), psychologist and author on relationships

Frost, Robert (1874–1963), American poet

Fuentes, Carlos (1928–2012), Mexican writer and diplomat

Fuller, R. Buckminster (1895–1983), American architect and engineer

Fuller, Thomas (1608–1661), English clergyman and author

Galbraith, John Kenneth (1908–2006), American economist and public official

Galilei, Galileo (1564–1642), Italian astronomer and physicist

Gandhi, Mohandas (1869–1948), Indian nonviolent nationalist

Garcia, Jerry (1942–1995), singer and songwriter for the Grateful Dead

Garis, Howard R. (1873–1962), American author, creator of the Uncle Wiggly series

Geisel, Theodor, *See* Seuss, Dr.

Gibbon, Edward (1737–1794), British historian

Gibran, Kahlil (1883–1931), Lebanese-American poet and novelist

Gide, André (1869–1951), French writer

Gilbert, Sir William S. (1836–1911), English playwright, librettist, and poet

Gladstone, William E. (1809–1898), British statesman

Goethe, Johann Wolfgang von (1749–1832), German poet, dramatist, and novelist

Goldsmith, Oliver (c. 1730–1774), British-Irish author and dramatist

Goldwater, Barry (1909–1998), U.S. senator

Goya, Francisco de (1746–1828), Spanish painter

Gracián, Baltasar (1601–1658), Spanish writer and philosopher

Graham, Billy (b. 1918), American evangelical preacher

Graham, Martha (1894–1991), American modern dancer and choreographer

Greene, Graham (1904–1991), English novelist and playwright

Gretzky, Wayne (b. 1961), Canadian hockey player

Guevara, Ernesto "Che" (1928–1967), Cuban revolutionary leader

Guthrie, Woody (1912–1967), American folk singer and composer

Hagen, Walter (1892–1969), American golfer

Hamilton, Lee (b. 1931), American congressman and 9/11 Commission chairman

Hamilton, Scott (b. 1958), American figure skater

Hammarskjöld, Dag (1905–1961), secretary-general of the United Nations

Hand, Learned (1872–1961), judge of the U.S. Court of Appeals

Harburg, E. Y. (1898–1981), American composer

Hardy, Thomas (1840–1928), English novelist

Harris, Sydney (1917–1986), American cartoonist and author

Harvey, Paul (1918–2009), American radio broadcaster

Hawking, Stephen (b. 1942), British theoretical physicist

Hawthorne, Nathaniel (1804–1864), American writer

Havel, Václav (1936–2011), Czech statesman and writer

Hazlitt, William (1778–1830), British essayist

Hecht, Ben (1894–1964), American writer

Hegel, Georg Wilhelm Friedrich (1770–1831), German philosopher

Hemingway, Ernest (1899–1961), American writer

Henry, Patrick (1736–1799), American statesman

Heraclitus (c. 535 BC–c. 475 BC), Greek philosopher

Herodotus (c. 484 BC–c. 425 BC), Greek historian

Hesse, Hermann (1877–1962), German novelist and poet

Hill, Napoleon (1883–1970), American entrepreneur and author

Hillel, Rabbi, ancient Babylonian Jewish scholar

Hippocrates (460 BC–370 BC), Greek physician

Hoffer, Eric (1898–1983), American self-educated longshoreman and
    author

Holmes, Oliver Wendell Jr. (1841–1935), U.S. Supreme Court justice

Holtz, Lou (b. 1937), American college football coach

Homer, seventh-century BC Greek poet

Horace (65 BC–8 BC), Latin poet

Hoyle, Edmond (1672–1769), British writer

Hubbard, L. Ron (1911–1986), American science-fiction writer

Hughes, Charles Evans (1862–1948), associate justice of the U.S. Supreme Court

Hughes, Langston (1902–1967), American poet, playwright, and social activist

Hugo, Victor (1802–1825), French writer, poet, and dramatist

Hume, David (1711–1776), Scottish philosopher and historian

Humphrey, Hubert H. (1911–1978), U.S. vice president

Hutchins, Robert (1899–1977), American educator

Huxley, Aldous (1894–1963), British novelist

Ibsen, Henrik (1828–1906), Norwegian dramatist and poet

Ingersoll, Robert (1833–1899), American orator and lawyer

Jagger, Mick (b. 1943), English lead singer of the Rolling Stones

James, William (1842–1910), American psychologist and philosopher

Jefferson, Thomas (1743–1826), third U.S. president

John XXIII (1881–1963), Italian pope

Johnson, Jimmy (b. 1943), American football coach and TV commentator

Johnson, Samuel (1709–1784), English author

Joubert, Joseph (1754–1824), French moralist

Joyce, James (1882–1941), Irish novelist

Jung, Carl (1875–1961), Swiss psychiatrist

Juvenal (c. 60 AD–c. 140 AD), Roman satirist

Kafka, Franz (1883–1924), Bohemian novelist

Kaiser, Henry J. (1882–1967), American industrialist

Kant, Immanuel (1724–1804), German metaphysical philosopher

Kaye, Danny (1911–1987), American actor, singer, and comedian

Keats, John (1795–1821), English poet

Keller, Helen (1880–1968), American writer and lecturer

Kempis, Saint Thomas à (1380–1471), Dutch theologian

Kennedy, John F. (1917–1963), thirty-fifth U.S. president

Kennedy, Robert Francis (1925–1968), U.S. attorney general

Kenny, Elizabeth (1880–1952), Australian nurse and author

Khayyam, Omar, eleventh-century Persian poet and mathematician

Khrushchev, Nikita (1894–1971), Soviet Communist premier of the
     USSR

Kierkegaard, Søren (1813–1855), Danish philosopher

King, Martin Luther Jr. (1929–1968), American minister and civil
     rights activist

Laërtius, Diogenes, third-century BC Greek biographer

Lagerlöf, Selma (1858–1940), Swedish author

Landers, Ann (1918–2002), American advice columnist

Lao-Tzu, sixth-century BC Chinese philosopher

Lawrence, D. H. (1885–1930), British novelist

Lawrence, T. E. (1888–1935), British adventurer and soldier, known
     as Lawrence of Arabia

Le Guin, Ursula K. (b. 1929), American science fiction and fantasy
     author

Lee, Harper (1926–2016), American Pulitzer Prize-winning novelist

Lemmon, Jack (1925–2001), American actor

Lerner, Max (1902–1992), American journalist and educator

Lewis, C. S. (1898–1963), British writer

Lichtenberg, Georg Christoph (1742–1799), German physicist and satirist

Lilly, John (c. 1554–1606), English dramatist and prose writer

Lincoln, Abraham (1809–1865), sixteenth U.S. president

Lippman, Walter (1889–1974), American political journalist

Locke, John (1632–1704), English empirical philosopher

Lombardi, Vince (1913–1970), American football coach

Longfellow, Henry Wadsworth (1807–1882), American poet

Lorenz, Konrad (1903–1989), Austrian zoologist and ethologist

Louis C.K., stage name of Louis Székely (b. 1967), American comedian and filmmaker

Lowell, James Russell (1819–1891), American poet

Luther, Martin (1483–1546), German leader of the Protestant Reformation

MacArthur, Douglas (1880–1964), American general

Machiavelli, Niccolò (1469–1527), Italian Renaissance author and statesman

Mandela, Nelson (1918–2013), South African anti-apartheid leader and president

Mankiewicz, Joseph L. (1909–1993), American film director and
  producer

Mansfield, Katherine (1888–1923), British short-story writer

Mantle, Mickey (1931–1995), American baseball player for the New
  York Yankees

Marceau, Marcel (1923–2007), French mime

Maritain, Jacques (1882–1973), French philosopher

Marley, Bob (1945–1981), Jamaican reggae singer

Marquis, Donald Robert Perry (1878–1937), American journalist and
  cartoonist

Maslow, Abraham (1908–1970), American psychologist

Matisse, Henri (1869–1954), French painter and sculptor

Maugham, W. Somerset (1874–1956), English novelist

Maurois, André (1885–1967), French writer and biographer

Maxwell, John C. (b. 1947), American author and motivational
  speaker

May, Rollo (1909–1994), American psychologist

McAdoo, William G. (1863–1941), U.S. senator and cabinet official

McCartney, Paul (b. 1942), British singer/songwriter, member of the
  Beatles

McGinley, Phyllis (1905–1978), American poet

McMurtry, Larry (b. 1936), American author

Melville, Herman (1819–1891), American author

Mencken, H(enry) L(ouis) (1880–1956), American editor and critic

Menninger, Dr. Karl Augustus (1893–1900), American psychiatrist

Merton, Thomas (1915–1968), American religious writer

Michelangelo (1475–1564), Italian Renaissance artist

Mies van der Rohe, Ludwig (1886–1969), German-American
minimalist architect

Mill, John Stuart (1806–1873), British philosopher and economist

Miller, Henry (1891–1980), American writer

Milne, A. A. (1882–1956), English author

Milton, John (1608–1674), English poet

Mizner, Wilson (1876–1933), American screenwriter

Molière, pseudonym of Jean-Baptiste Poquelin (1622–1673), French
playwright

Monroe, Marilyn (1926–1962), American film actress

Morley, Christopher Darlington (1890–1957), American author and
editor

Morley, John, Viscount (1838–1923), British statesman

Moses, Anna Mary Robertson "Grandma" (1860–1961), American
painter

Murphy, Edward A. (1918–1990), Air Force engineer after whom
Murphy's Law is named

Murrow, Edward R. (1908–1965), American journalist and radio
broadcaster

Nathan, George Jean (1882–1958), American editor and writer

Nehru, Jawaharlal (1889–1964), first Indian prime minister

Newman, John Henry (1801–1890), British theologian

Newton, Sir Isaac (1642–1727), English mathematician and physicist

Nichols, Mike (1931–2014), German-American stage and film director

Niebuhr, Reinhold (1892–1971), American theologian

Nietzsche, Friedrich Wilhelm (1844–1900), German philosopher

Nightingale, Florence (1820–1910), English social reformer and founder of modern nursing

Nin, Anaïs (1903–1977), French-American writer

O'Neill, Thomas P. "Tip" Jr. (1912–1994), speaker of the U.S. House of Representatives

O'Rourke, P. J. (b. 1947) American political satirist

Obama, Barack (b. 1961), forty-fourth U.S. president

Occam, William of (c. 1285–c. 1349), English philosopher

Ortega y Gasset, José (1883–1955), Spanish author

Orwell, George (1903–1950), British novelist and essayist

Ovid (43 BC–17 AD), Roman poet

Paddleford, Clementine (1898–1967), American food editor

Paige, Satchel (1906–1982), American baseball player

Paine, Thomas (1737–1809), Anglo-American political theorist

Parkinson, Cyril Northcote (1909–1993), British historian

Parks, Rosa (1913–2005), American civil rights activist

Pascal, Blaise (1623–1662), French philosopher

Pasteur, Louis (1822–1895), French chemist

Paton, Alan (1903–1988), South African novelist

Patton, George Smith Jr. (1885–1945), American military leader

Peale, Norman Vincent (1898–1993), American clergyman

Penney, James Cash (1875–1971), American merchant entrepreneur

Pericles (495 BC–429 BC), Athenian statesman

Perot, H. Ross (b. 1930), American business executive and
presidential candidate

Peter, Laurence J. (1919–1990), American educator and writer

Peters, Thomas (1738–1792), Revolutionary War–era loyalist and
leader of freed slaves

Phelps, William Lyon (1865–1943), U.S. educator and literary critic

Phillips, Wendell (1811–1884), American reformer and speaker

Picasso, Pablo (1881–1973), Spanish artist

Pittacus (c. 650 BC–c. 570 BC), Greek statesman and military leader

Plato (c. 427 BC–347 BC), Greek philosopher

Plautus (c. 254 BC–184 BC), Roman writer of comedies

Plutarch (c. 46 AD–c. 120 AD), Greek philosopher and biographer

Polybius (c. 203 BC–c. 120 BC), Greek historian

Pope, Alexander (1688–1744), English poet and satirist

Pound, Ezra (1885–1972), American poet

Powell, Colin (b. 1937), U.S. military figure and secretary of state

Priest, Ivy Baker (1905–1975), treasurer of the United States

Proust, Marcel (1871–1922), French writer

Pythagoras, sixth-century BC Greek mathematician and philosopher

Rand, Ayn (1905–1982), Russian-American novelist

Randolph, A. Philip (1889–1979), American civil rights leader

Reagan, Ronald (1911–2004), fortieth U.S. president

Reuther, Walter (1907–1970), American labor leader

Rice, Grantland (1880–1954), American sportswriter

Richards, Keith (b. 1943), English guitarist/singer for the Rolling
    Stones

Richter, Jean Paul Friedrich (1763–1825), German writer

Rickey, Branch (1881–1965), American baseball executive

Rickover, Hyman George (1900–1986), American admiral

Rilke, Rainer Maria (1875–1926), German poet

Robbins, Tony (b. 1960), leadership consultant and trainer

Rockefeller, John D. Jr. (1874–1960), American oil magnate and
    philanthropist

Rodin, Auguste (1840–1917), French sculptor

Rogers, Roy (1911–1998), American Western movie actor

Rogers, Will (1879–1935), American humorist

Rohn, Jim (1930–2009), American motivational speaker

Rollins, Henry (b. 1961), American punk singer

Rooney, Andrew A. "Andy" (1919–2011), American TV personality

Roosevelt, Eleanor (1884–1962), American first lady and diplomat

Roosevelt, Franklin Delano (1882–1945), thirty-second U.S.
    president

Roosevelt, James (1907–1991), son of Franklin D. Roosevelt

Roosevelt, Theodore (1858–1919), twenty-sixth U.S. president

Rosten, Leo C. (1908–1997), Polish-American writer

Rousseau, Jean-Jacques (1712–1778), French philosopher

Rowling, J. K. (b. 1965), British author of the Harry Potter series

Rubin, Theodore Isaac (b. 1923), American psychiatrist and author

Runyon, Damon (1880–1946), American short-story writer and
    humorist

Ruskin, John (1819–1900), British art critic

Russell, Bertrand (1872–1970), British philosopher and
    mathematician

Russell, Rosalind (1907–1976), American actress

Saadi (1184–1291), Persian mystic poet

Safire, William (1929–2009), American journalist and speechwriter

Sagan, Carl (1934–1996), American astronomer

Saigyō Hōshi (1118–1190), Japanese poet

Saint-Exupéry, Antoine de (1900–1944), French writer

Salinger, J. D. (1919–2010), American novelist and short-story writer

Salk, Jonas (1914–1995), American physician and microbiologist

Sandburg, Carl (1878–1967), American writer and poet

Santayana, George (1863–1952), American philosopher and poet

Saroyan, William (1908–1981), American author and 1939 Pulitzer
    Prize winner

Sartre, Jean-Paul (1905–1980), French philosopher

Savile, George (1633–1695), English statesman

Schuller, Robert H. (1926–2015), American Protestant minister

Schwab, Charles (1862–1939), American steel magnate

Schweitzer, Albert (1875–1965), Swiss theologian, missionary, and
    Nobel Prize winner

Scott, Sir Walter (1771–1832), Scottish poet

Scowcroft, General Brent (b. 1925), American military and political
    figure

Seattle, Chief (c. 1784–1866), chief of the Suquamish tribe

Seneca the Elder (c. 60 BC–c. 37 AD), Roman rhetorician and writer

Seneca, Lucius Annaeus (the Younger) (c. 4 BC–65 AD), Roman
    stoic philosopher

Seuss, Dr. (Theodor Geisel) (1904–1991), American children's book
    author

Sewell, Anna (1820–1878), English author of *Black Beauty*

Shakespeare, William (1564–1616), English dramatist

Shaw, George Bernard (1856–1950), Irish dramatist and critic

Shedd, John A. (1859–1928), American educator

Sheehy, Gail (b. 1937), American editor and journalist

Shelley, Percy Bysshe (1792–1822), British romantic poet

Sholem Aleichem, pen name of Solomon Naumovich Rabinovich
    (1859–1916), Yiddish author and playwright

Singer, Isaac Bashevis (1904–1991), American novelist

Sivananda, Swami (1887–1963), Indian physician and sage

Smiles, Samuel (1812–1904), writer

Smith, Betty (1896–1972), American author

Smith, Logan Pearsall (1865–1946), American essayist

Smith, Margaret Chase (1897–1995), U.S. senator

Socrates (469 BC–399 BC), Greek philosopher

Solon (c. 639 BC–c. 559 BC), Athenian statesman, lawgiver, and
reformer

Solzhenitsyn, Aleksandr (1918–2008), Russian writer

Sondheim, Stephen (b. 1930), American composer

Sophocles (c. 496 BC–406 BC), Greek dramatist

Spencer, Herbert (1820–1903), British evolutionary philosopher

Spenser, Edmund (c. 1552–1599), English poet

Spock, Benjamin (1903–1998), American pediatrician and educator

St. Jerome (c. 347–420), Early Christian scholar

St. John, Henry (1678–1751), British politician and author

Stalin, Joseph (1879–1953), Soviet leader

Standing Bear, Luther (Ota Kte, Mochunozhin) (1868–1939), Oglala
Sioux chief

Stanley, Edward (1826–1893), British statesman

Stanton, Elizabeth Cady (1815–1902), American reformer and
woman suffragist

Steichen, Edward (1879–1973), American photographer

Stein, Ben (b. 1944), American economist and TV personality

Stein, Gertrude (1874–1946), American experimental writer

Steinbeck, John (1902–1968), American novelist

Steinem, Gloria (b. 1934), American feminist writer and editor

Stengel, Charles "Casey," (1890–1975), American baseball legend

Stevenson, Adlai E. (1900–1965), American statesman

Stevenson, Robert Louis (1850–1894), British novelist

Stowe, Harriet Beecher (1811–1896), American writer

Sumner, Charles (1811–1874), U.S. senator from Massachusetts

Swedenborg, Emanuel (1688–1772), Swedish scientist, religious
    teacher, and mystic

Swift, Jonathan (1667–1745), English writer

Syrus, Publilius (b. 42 AD), Roman writer

Tagore, Rabindranath (1861–1941), Indian poet and author

Teasdale, Sara (1884–1933), American poet

Tennyson, Alfred Lord (1809–1892), English poet

Terence (c. 185 BC–159 BC), Roman writer of comedies

Teresa, Mother (1910–1997), Albanian-Indian missionary, Nobel
    Peace Prize winner

Thackeray, William Makepeace (1811–1863), British author

Thatcher, Margaret (1925–2013), British prime minister

Thoreau, Henry David (1817–1862), American author and naturalist

Thucydides (c. 460 BC–c. 400 BC), Greek historian of Athens

Thurber, James (1894–1961), American writer and cartoonist

Tolstoy, Leo (1828–1910), Russian novelist and philosopher

Tomlin, Lily (b. 1939), American actress and comedian

Toynbee, Arnold Joseph (1889–1975), British historian

Trollope, Anthony (1815–1882), English novelist

Truman, Harry S. (1884–1972), thirty-third U.S. president

Twain, Mark, pseudonym of Samuel L. Clemens (1835–1910), American author

Updike, John (1932–2009), American novelist and critic

Valéry, Paul (1871–1945), French poet

Van Dyke, Henry (1852–1933), American Presbyterian clergyman

van Gogh, Vincent (1853–1890), Dutch Post-Impressionist painter

Vidal, Gore (1925–2012), American author and critic

Virgil (70 BC–19 BC), Roman poet

Voltaire, pseudonym of François-Marie Arouet (1694–1778), French philosopher

von Bismarck, Otto (1815–1898), German chancellor

von Braun, Wernher (1912–1977), German-American engineer

Vonnegut, Kurt (1922–2007), American author

Waitley, Denis (b. 1933), American motivational speaker

Walker, Alice (b. 1944), American novelist

Wallace, David Foster (1962–2008), American writer and teacher

Walpole, Horace (1717–1797), English author

Walton, Sam (1918–1992), American businessman, founder of Wal-Mart

Ward, William Arthur (1921–1994), American writer

Warhol, Andy (1928–1987), American pop artist

Washington, Booker T. (1865–1915), American educator and writer

Washington, George (1732–1799), First U.S. president

Watson, Thomas J. Sr. (1874–1956), American business leader, IBM chairman

Watts, Alan B. (1915–1973), American philosopher and author

Wayne, John (1907–1979), American film actor

Webster, Daniel (1782–1852), American congressman

Welles, Orson (1915–1985), American actor, director, and producer

Wells, H. G. (1866–1946), English author

White, E. B. (1899–1985), American writer

White, T. H. (1915–1986), American political journalist

Whitehead, Alfred North (1861–1947), British mathematician and philosopher

Whitman, Walt (1819–1892), American poet

Whittier, John Greenleaf (1807–1892), American poet

Wiesel, Elie (1928–2016), writer and Holocaust survivor

Wilde, Oscar (1854–1900), Irish dramatist

Wilder, Thornton (1897–1975), American novelist and dramatist

Will, George F. (b. 1941), American political journalist

Williams, Jimmy (1917–1993), American horse trainer

Williams, Tennessee (1911–1983), American dramatist

Wilson, Woodrow (1856–1924), twenty-eighth U.S. president

Winfrey, Oprah (b. 1954), American talk show host and producer

Wooden, John R. (b. 1910), American basketball coach

Woolf, Virginia (1882–1941), English novelist and essayist

Woollcott, Alexander (1887–1943), American critic and journalist

Wordsworth, William (1770–1850), British romantic poet

Wright, Frank Lloyd (1867–1959), American architect

Wright, Leonard, American fly-fisher

Wright, Steven (b. 1955), American comedian

Yeats, William Butler (1865–1939), Irish poet

Young, Brigham (1801–1877), American Mormon leader

Yutang, Lin (1895–1976), Chinese-American writer, translator, and
   editor

Zapata, Emiliano (c. 1879–1919), Mexican revolutionary

Zola, Émile (1840–1902), French novelist